LIVING HERITAGE

LIVING
HERITAGE
CENTURIES IN BUSINESS

SABINA R. KORFMANN-BODENMANN

SHOWCASE
Roli Books

SHOWCASE
A Roli Books imprint for titles sponsored by individuals or organisations.

ISBN: 978-93-5194-178-1

© Sabina R. Korfmann-Bodenmann, 2016
© Book concept, layout, and design: Roli Books, 2016

Published in India by Roli Books
M-75, Greater Kailash II Market
New Delhi-110 048, India.
Phone: ++91-11-40682000
Email: info@rolibooks.com
Website: www.rolibooks.com

Design: Sneha Pamneja
Editor: Neelam Narula
Layout: Naresh L. Mondal
Pre-press: Jyoti Dey
Production: Yuvraj Singh

Printed and bound in India

CONTENTS

To the Love of my Life

FOREWORD

*H*eritage may be an old-fashioned word, but its value is current: it is the essence of who we are, and there is no shortcut to that.

This book features companies and institutions, which have been active for at least two hundred years. The variety of companies presented is broad, and the organizational forms are diverse; some are still family-owned whilst others have different ownership structures.

These include leaders in their fields who have set industry standards, and are looked upon with respect. They have influenced the way we think. They have contributed to our aesthetic sense, and pursued new commercial paths. In addition, they often were – and still are – important economic agents for whole regions.

The founders and successors have accepted the responsibilities they've inherited with their positions. They are pioneers and leaders, and their employees reflect these values by taking a special pride in the company for which they work. Both, owners and employees, are infused with passion.

The different environmental and historical circumstances make them experienced survivors. They adapt to new market conditions, not only by expanding their range of business activities or geographically but also by focusing on what they are doing best. There is a fine line between honouring the past and reflecting the Zeitgeist!

"Every time I take a step towards preserving the past, it puts me a step forward into the future. A future that will make us want to look back and walk ahead with pride."

SHRIJI ARVIND SINGH MEWAR OF UDAIPUR

Antinori

ITALY

One of the ten oldest family businesses in the world, Antinori frequently shook up the Italian wine industry with innovations, leading to far-reaching changes in rules and attitudes.

1385

The Antinori family has been involved in the production of wine for over six centuries, ever since Giovanni di Piero Antinori entered the *Arte Fiorentina*, the Winemakers' Guild of the city of Florence, in 1385. For twenty-six generations, the family has managed the business with courageous and innovative decisions, always maintaining a fundamental respect for tradition, and for the territories in which it operates.

The family responded to the inflation of the 1980s and 1990s with a programme of investment in wineries and vineyards, most notably the Atlas Peak winery in California, and 325 hectares around Badia a Passignano in Tuscany. It also expanded into the Piedmont and Puglia regions, and entered into joint ventures in the USA, Chile, Hungary, Malta and Romania. Antinori presently owns 1,742 hectares of vineyards in Italy, and 2,358 hectares in other countries.

Since its foundation, the Antinori family has been part of PFV (*Premium Familiae Vini*), an informal association of winemaking houses, which belong to families. Today, the firm is run by Marchese Piero Antinori, with the support of his three daughters, who are directly involved in managing the business. In recent years, the Antinori brand has expanded beyond wine, though still with an emphasis on Tuscan classics: oil, country inns, restaurants and stores.

We have a mission which has not yet been fulfilled. It drives us to develop the vast potential of our vineyards, and to reconcile both new discoveries yet to be made, and the heritage of Tuscan taste. The Tuscan heritage includes tradition, culture, agriculture, art and literature, all of which fuse in the identity of the Marchesi Antinori firm, whose major character trait is that of being fundamentally Tuscan.

MARCHESA ALBIERA ANTINORI
Vice President

Rinuccio di Antinori is recorded as making wine at the Castello di Combiate near the Tuscan town of Calenzano in 1180. When the *castello* was destroyed in 1202, the family moved to Florence where they became involved in silk-weaving and banking. In the mid-fifteenth century, the Antinori family was one of the most important in the city, being politically active, and friends of the most influential local personalities including the Medici. However, like many Florentines, the family was bankrupted by the ravages of Charles V of Spain, and the economic effect of his New World gold. Nonetheless, the family prospered in the ensuing peace and gained the title of Marchese from the House of Habsburg-Lorraine in the eighteenth century.

• • •

In 1904, the first Gran Spumante Marchese Antinori was made: it was called *Cordon Rouge*. But sparkling wine can be volatile. One morning, several years later, about seven-thousand bottles exploded in the San Casciano wine cellars. The French expert the family had called in specifically to oversee the wine had made a serious mistake (and was swiftly sent packing). This event led to a vociferous family argument over sparkling wine. Eventually, a new winemaker from France was hired. Unlike his predecessor, he proved to be worth his salt. The Antinoris don't give up easily and indeed, years after those early efforts with bubbles, they have become one of the top producers of high-quality Italian sparkling wines today.

• • •

Niccolo Antinori scandalised Tuscany in 1924 by making a Chianti containing Bordeaux grape varieties. He continued to experiment with new blends, types of barrels, temperature control and bottle aging. He retired in 1966 to be replaced by his son Piero. Piero, even more innovative, tested early harvesting of white grapes, types of barrels, stainless-steel vats, and malolactic fermentation of red wines. The real revolution came in 1971 with Tignanello, a barrel-aged wine from the eponymous vineyard that had both Cabernet Sauvignon and Cabernet Franc varieties, which meant that it was not eligible for the Chianti Classico appellation. Tignanello shook up the Italian wine industry leading to far-reaching changes in rules and attitudes.

• • •

The Antinori family has developed a business philosophy over the years that they call the "Six Ps":
Patience: The slow and thoughtful pace of grape-growing and winemaking are a challenge given the frantic pace of the current business environment. Albiera Antinori says, "Today, we have high-speed aeroplanes and high-speed trains, and thoughts and words travel even more quickly on the Web. But wine still develops at the same pace. You can't make it go any faster."
Perseverance: A classic Tuscan trait. Without "trying and trying again", there would be no Tignanello or Solaia today.
Planning: The only tool that can be used to deal with the unforeseeable aspects of the wine business. One tills the soil, plants vines, schedules harvests, has the cellars ready with new barrels and bottles, and then something goes wrong. It's inevitable!
Precision: A winemaker's expertise is a mix of perfectionism and practice.
Profit: Part of the business, for sure, but profit is also proof of efficiency. It confirms that the wines were produced the right way, meet the needs of customers, and are better than competitors' wines.
Passion: A way of approaching life, passion represents everything the Antinoris do.

• • •

From the highway, one can miss Antinori's new headquarters, the building hidden from full view, buried literally inside a hill. Once inside, the space unfolds as a series of surprises. The building is constructed from indigenous materials, with sustainability in mind. A snaking driveway deposits visitors into an underground parking area. From here, visitors ascend the tour-de-force corkscrew staircase made of rust-coloured steel, which twists upwards like a large-scale sculpture. It pops through one of the circular openings onto the terrace, almost the length of a football pitch. Behind a two-storey glass wall lie the offices, museum, shop and tasting rooms, which are theatrically cantilevered over the wine cellars. These are a series of sleek caves as big and sombre as cathedrals — spectacular rooms tucked deep inside the hill and hidden behind discreet doors. The hill keeps the cellars naturally temperate. A factory and office complex doesn't have to be a cheap mirrored-glass box or a trumped-up Renaissance villa. It can be Architecture with a capital A. That is the Antinoris' message.

Joh. Barth & Sohn, Hops Traders

GERMANY

Eight generations of the same family have made the company the leader in hops trading and processing worldwide.

1794

Eight generations of the same family have led the company since it was founded by Johann Barth.

Joh. Barth & Sohn leads the hops trade and hops processing in Germany, marketing more than a third of the German hops harvest. The company is also number one worldwide with the Barth-Haas Group of companies, selling around 35 per cent of all the hops harvested worldwide.

While Joh. Barth & Sohn used to focus its business activities on the hops trade to the exclusion of all else, hops processing has become a second focus over the past several decades. Potential uses for hops other than in the brewing industry, particularly in food and dietary supplements, are becoming increasingly significant.

PULL THE RING → ← FOR CRAFT BEER

CREW

Republic

HANDCRAFTED
BEER FROM
München

BOTTLES
0.33L

PULL THE RING → ← FOR CRAFT BEER

CREW

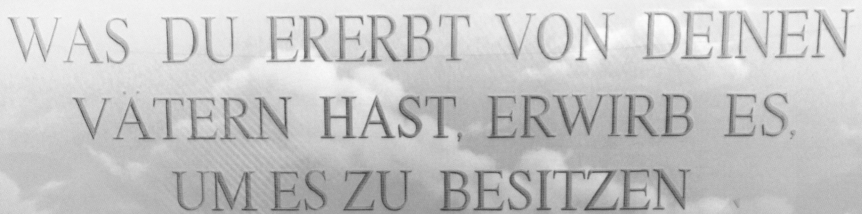

WAS DU ERERBT VON DEINEN
VÄTERN HAST, ERWIRB ES,
UM ES ZU BESITZEN

In 1994, Joh. Barth & Sohn celebrated its 200th jubilee as the world leader in the hops industry. True to its motto, "Was Du ererbt von Deinen Vätern hast, erwirb es, um es zu besitzen" (to really own what you have inherited from your ancestors, you must earn it again yourself), each generation has contributed to this achievement. They have done this primarily thanks to the cohesion of the family and its members' business acumen, as well as their readiness to reinvest the profits from the business. This alone made it possible to emerge stronger than ever from political and economic turmoil.

STEPHAN J. BARTH
Managing Partner

The ancestors of the Barth family were mostly craftsmen and farmers; they shared the vicissitudes of Franconia, a region not particularly blessed by nature. They were industrious, poor, had many children, and were – *cuius regio, eius religio* – Protestant.

• • •

Hops trading at the end of the eighteenth century was conducted by traders who took their merchandise along on covered wagons, and offered it by the pound to the numerous small breweries along the road. If Georg Barth had delivered to the customer the previous year, he used the visit for the purpose of collecting payment for the previous year's delivery, which was the equivalent of a payment term of twelve months. Thus the level of sales was tied to his own financial capacity.

• • •

In 1858, Johann Barth transferred the firm to Nuremberg, the recognised centre of the hops trade. The lifting of the restriction against the use of sulphur for export hops only in Central Franconia provided important advantages for the hops trade in and around Nuremberg.

• • •

The Annual Hops Report, now an institution, was begun during the 1870s. The oldest copy dates back to 1878. Since there were no official statistics for many decades, the rapidly expanding international trade in hops meant that there was a considerable interest on all sides in objective reporting and presentation of figures. At an early stage, Joh. Barth & Sohn made attempts to publish international hops and beer statistics, to determine the worldwide supply and demand. Over the course of the years, reporting was refined and expanded and published in its current form as a final crop and market report.

• • •

The National Socialist government, which came to power in 1933, implemented its doctrine of a controlled and self-sufficient economy. Hops were placed under the umbrella of the Reichsnährstand (meaning roughly national nutrition authority). Cultivation of acreage was controlled, the purchase and sales prices were set by officials, and export prices were lowered by subsidies based on a complicated system of country-oriented prices. These subsidies had to be funded by the industry itself through higher domestic prices. The only freedom in this strongly-regulated economy was the free selection of buyers and sellers.

• • •

At the beginning of the 1950s, a series of structural changes were introduced which changed German hops trading fundamentally, and had a considerable impact on Joh. Barth & Sohn.

Mechanization of hops growing: The ever-increasing shortage of hops-pickers meant that new ways of harvesting had to be found. In 1955, the first picking machine was put into operation. By 1964, 95 per cent of hops were harvested by machine; in 1967 picking by hand belonged to a romantic past.

Forward contracts: Since the resumption of a free market in 1949, hops prices, which were always paid after the harvest, were subject to considerable fluctuation. The growing German harvest also made it more difficult and risky to manage purchase and sales during the few months of the season. The high investments accompanying the mechanisation of hops cultivation stimulated the desire for security on the part of producers. In 1957, Joh. Barth & Sohn came up with the idea of introducing a system of fixed prices with growers and breweries based on multi-year delivery contracts.

New varieties: Although the standard Hallertau Mittelfrüh variety had been grown successfully for decades, it had shown an increasing susceptibility to the wilt disease. At the same time, the brewing industry worldover became interested in more bitter hops. In 1959, roots of Northern Brewer hops were introduced experimentally. They met expectations not only in increased bitter resin content, but were also more resistant to the wilt disease. As late as 1993, 27.5 per cent of all German hops planted were of the Northern Brewer variety.

Hops products: Hops extracts produced by means of solvents had already been in the market since the 1920s, but had attracted relatively little attention. With the rapid increase in worldwide beer output, technological progress in the brewing industry, and advanced research analysing the components of hops, a growing interest on the part of the international brewing industry could no longer be ignored.

Berenberg Bank

GERMANY

The Bank has had 38 personally-liable partners who have ensured continuity in the business for over 425 years.

1590

Hans and Paul Berenberg, religious refugees from the Netherlands, founded their company in Hamburg. They were active in the cloth trade, and dealt in general imports and exports.

1684

Cornelius Berenberg was the first Berenberg to take the oath as a citizen. In doing so, he made it possible for future generations to work in all public offices. Unlike in other cities, government positions were not reserved for the oldest families. Immigrant families were able to take on official functions relatively quickly, as long as they had their own home and capital assets.

1756–63

The Seven Years' War, which involved half of Europe, brought significant advantages for the Hamburg economy. Through a constant need for financing of the warring nations, the currency in circulation was expanded dramatically. However, at the end of the war, the commodities business abruptly declined. Trade in bills of exchange also collapsed and many banks and companies went bankrupt. The Berenbergs' company also ran into difficulties, and had to be supported by the loan fund that had rapidly been set up and with which the city council helped generally healthy companies to cope with temporary illiquidity.

19th Century

Trade boomed in the Hanseatic city. The increasing significance of maritime trade and industry was reflected in the founding of many new joint stock companies. At this time Joh. Berenberg, Gossler & Co was among the founders of Hapag (1847), the Norddeutscher Lloyd (1857), the Ilseder Hütte (1858), the Norddeutsche Versicherungs-AG (1857), and the Vereinsbank in Hamburg (1856). The bank was active abroad, becoming, among other things, a founding shareholder in Bergens Privatbank in Bergen (1855), the Hong Kong and Shanghai Banking Corporation HSBC (1865), the Danske Landmandsbank in Copenhagen (1871), and the Svenska Handelsbanken Stockholm (1871).

2015

The company is celebrating 425 years in business. During these years, Berenberg was led by thirty-eight personally liable partners.

At the end of the sixteenth century, Dutch Protestants were confronted with the choice of either converting to Catholicism or leaving the country, and the Protestant Berenbergs left Antwerp, then the richest and busiest city in Europe, in search of a new home. They found it in Hamburg, where they founded their company in 1590. The company was active in trading cloth, grains, spices, and salt. The Dutch Protestants were quite openly ambitious and successful. At the beginning of the seventeenth century, of the forty-two companies in Hamburg with a turnover of over 100,000 marks, thirty-two were of Dutch origin. At first, the Dutch were subject to certain restrictions. For example, they were not allowed to do business with other foreigners within the city's borders. Foreign traders were later put on an equal footing with the citizens of Hamburg.

• • •

In the absence of a working banking system, merchants used to take on the financing of commodity trading themselves. They granted their customers credit and paid their suppliers advances on their shipments. The great number of different currencies also offered the basis for a comprehensive exchange business with good earnings potential. The Berenbergs also increased the assets purchased by underwriting financial transactions, and increasingly working as bankers.

• • •

In 175 years, five generations of the Berenberg family had given their name to the company, and it had become successful with the passing of time. In 1768, the sole heir was Johann Berenberg's only daughter Elisabeth. To secure the continued existence of the company after his death, Johann Berenberg looked for a new partner. He found one in Johann Hinrich Gossler, the son of a family who had been based in Hamburg since the fourteenth century. Gossler had learned the trade with the Berenbergs. He asked for Elisabeth Berenberg's hand, and they married in 1768, shortly before he became a partner in the firm, which was renamed "Johann Berenberg & Gossler".

• • •

At the time of the foundation of the German Reich in 1871, John Berenberg-Gossler had been a partner in the banking house for six years. Among the merchants of the Hanseatic cities Hamburg and Bremen, there were considerable reservations about the potential impact of the founding of the Reich on trade. Hamburg eventually entered into a customs union with the German Reich in 1888, but not without a long drawn-out dispute. Unlike many of his peers, John Berenberg-Gossler energetically championed the customs union, as well as plans for a free port for Hamburg. To make place for the new port, entire neighbourhoods of the city were demolished and relocated; around 24,000 people were resettled. The Speicherstadt was built, an unmistakable monument to the Hanseatic entrepreneurial spirit, a solid red-brick commercial Gothic construction built on oak piles close to the water; it is still the largest warehouse complex of its kind and unique among world heritage sites.

• • •

In recognition of his service, he was raised to the Prussian nobility in 1889, and was made a hereditary baron in 1910. He was mocked in Hamburg (Mayor Buchard: "A Hamburg merchant simply cannot be ennobled"), and his family was concerned (John's sister Susanne Amsinck: "But John, think of our good name!"), but the title was an advantage outside of Hamburg.

• • •

After the First World War, the German Reich was in tatters. The economy recovered slowly and laboriously. In 1920, at Christmas, the employees of the Berenberg Company received a package with flour, rice, bacon, and other food. Inflation became hyperinflation, and a pound of butter cost forty million Reichsmarks. In the German Reich, 135 printers and thirty-five paper factories worked on producing new bank notes; in the Berenberg bank, 400 employees were tasked with testing and counting the newly printed money. Printing all those noughts created jobs!

• • •

The company survived Nazi rule as a holding company in which the companies' many activities were combined. Many diary entries document Baron Cornelius von Berenberg-Gossler's outright rejection of National Socialism. After the annexation of the Sudetenland and of Austria, he wrote in 1938: "Rather a small, properly governed state than such a big empire, as Germany is today, without law or decency, with a government of thieves and murderers." On 3 May 1945, as British troops marched into Hamburg, the seventy-one year old wrote in his diary: "Now we must be ready for the consequences of the war, and gradually try to help the children to build their futures."

Pietro Beretta, Fabbrica d'Armi

ITALY

The oldest manufacturer of competition and military firearms has become a trademark for precision weapons today.

1526

The Beretta Company was mentioned in a document for the first time, when the Venetian gunsmith Bartolomeo Beretta received a large order from the city's arsenal. This makes Beretta the oldest armaments manufacturer in the world. Since almost half a millennium, the company was passed down, uninterrupted, through fifteen generations of Berettas.

Today

The Beretta Holding Group, established in 1995, participates directly or indirectly in twenty-six companies. Over the years, the Group has progressively expanded its range of products, including:
- Hunting: A focal point for hunting enthusiasts worldwide.
- Sporting: From amateur to professional and Olympic level.
- Clothing and Accessories: The clothing and accessories line is tailored to the world of hunting, shooting, and outdoor activities.
- Opto-Electronics: Through major acquisitions, the Group has also entered the field of optics, scopes, and binoculars.
- Defence and Law Enforcement: A key partner of governments worldwide as it is a supplier of integrated solutions utilised by defence departments and law enforcement agencies.

The Beretta Holding Group has approximately 3,000 employees, and an annual turnover in excess of 600 million Euros.

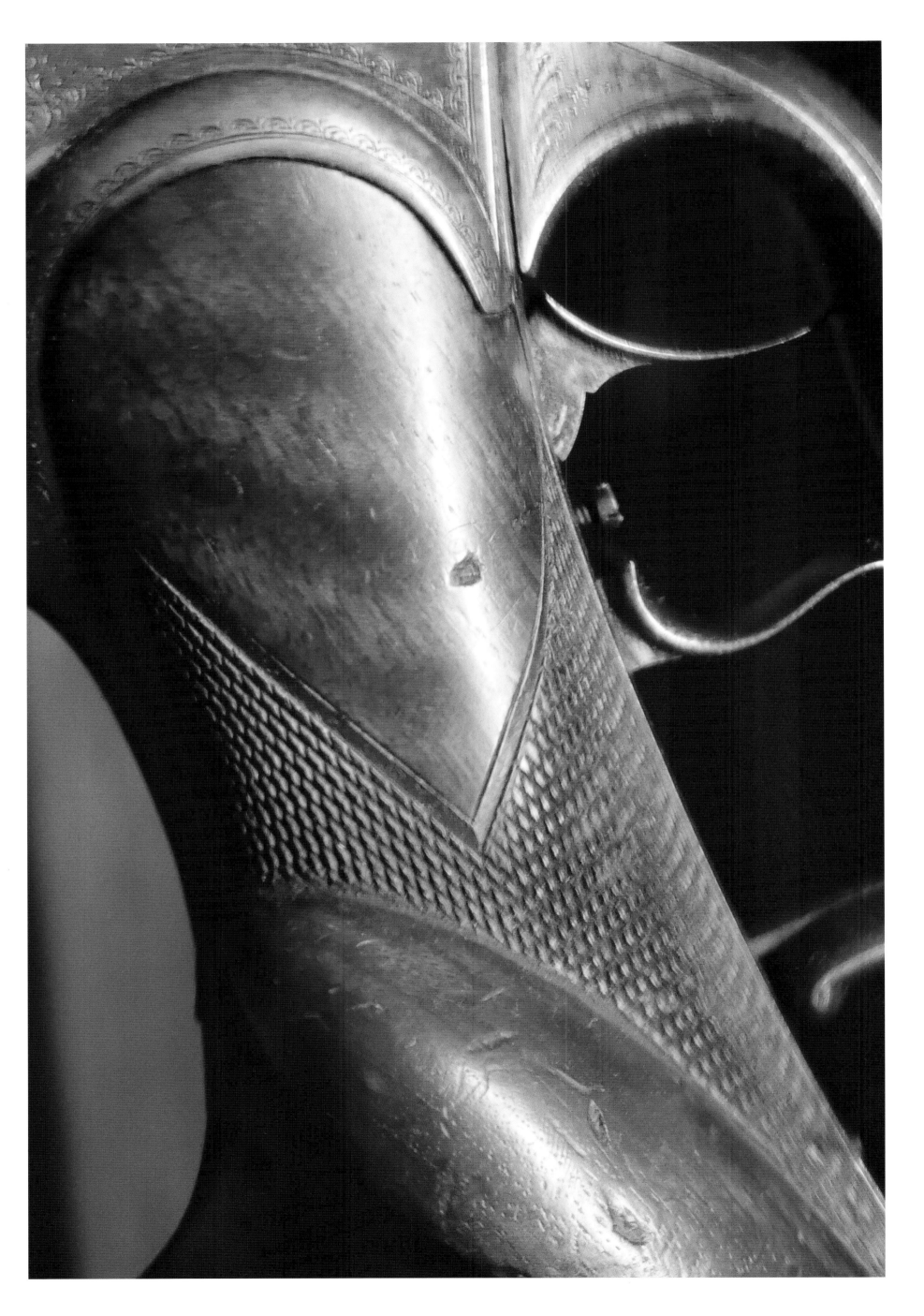

Industriousness, inventiveness, traditional methods, attention to the needs of its customers and its craftsmen, as well as ongoing research, technological improvement, and state-of-the-art manufacturing methods are the foundation on which Beretta has built its image. Since 1526, its competition and military firearms have established the trademark of this historic gun manufacturer.

UGO GUSSALLI BERETTA
Chief Executive Officer

Beretta's output is approximately 1,500 weapons a day, and covers just about the entire range of portable weapons: over-and-under and side-by-side rifles for hunting and competition in different calibres and finish grades, semiautomatic rifles and carbines, express double rifles, semiautomatic pistols, and assault rifles. An estimated 90 per cent of Beretta's production consists of sporting firearms, with more than 75 per cent of its arms being exported to about one hundred countries.

• • •

Beretta has been supplying firearms to the armed forces and police services of Italy and other countries for many years. So successful have the pistols been that the American armed forces and state police services started using the Beretta 92 series (one of which is the well-known Beretta 92FS 9mm Parabellum, also known as M9) in 1985. Subsequently, the French National Gendarmerie and Air Force also opted for a similar solution.

From the beginning of the twenty-first century, orders for the Beretta 92 series included contracts for the supply of 45,000 pistols to the Spanish Guardia Civil, about 40,000 pistols to the Turkish national police force, and almost 580,000 pistols for the US armed forces (including the largest US military handgun contract since the Second World War).

• • •

Beretta's success in the defence and law enforcement fields is matched by its success in competitive shooting sports. The first Olympic gold medal won with a Beretta was in clay pigeon shooting in Melbourne in 1956, followed by frequent victories in major international competitions. Medals were won with Berettas at the Olympic Games of Rome (1960), Munich (1972), Montreal (1976), Moscow (1980), Los Angeles (1984), Seoul (1988), Barcelona (1992), Atlanta (1996), Sydney (2000), Athens (2004), and Beijing (2008). At the London 2012 Olympic Games, confirmation of Beretta's sports vocation came in the form of one gold, one silver, and one bronze medal. More international competitions have been won with Beretta competition guns than with any other brand.

• • •

The Beretta Trident Programme is the first and only system to rate shooting sports venues. Not an endorsement for purchase, Tridents are awarded for excellence – like Michelin stars are for restaurants. While emphasising the outstanding hunting or shooting experience, the evaluation system recognizes, and rates everything from the food on the table to dog kennels. A Beretta Trident venue represents the best of the best, with only 5 per cent of destinations worldwide considered good enough to merit even one Trident.

One Trident indicates that a shooting sports venue is among the top end of similar venues around the world: its available amenities and activities are all of exceedingly high quality.

Two Tridents include all the assets of a One Trident, plus a superlative selection of programmes and amenities at quality levels far exceeding industry standards.

Three Tridents include all the assets of a One and Two Trident location and indicates the pinnacle of shooting sports venues.

{Pietro Beretta, Fabbrica d'Armi}

Tessitura Bevilacqua
ITALY

Since the eighteenth century, this house of weavers has been synonymous with Venetian velvet.

14th Century

Velvet, from the Latin *vellus* (fleece), conjures up visions of sumptuousness, refined luxury, and soft, sensual silk material ideal for both clothing and furnishings. Produced using various techniques since antiquity, the type best known today dates back to fourteenth-century Venice. The tradition of Venetian velvet is synonymous with Tessitura Bevilacqua.

18th Century

According to family records, the Bevilacqua's were active in weaving since the eighteenth century, but only formed a company in 1875 as evidenced by the inscription on an Istrian stone set at the entrance to Calle Bembo: "*Per l'arte della seta Bevilacqua MDCCCLXXV*" (For the Bevilacqua silk makers).

Today

Various management positions in the business are held by members of the Bevilacqua family: Rodolfo, Alberto and Mario. Mario's son, Emanuele, has taken such a keen interest in the history and techniques of the family company that he has conducted specialist studies on the old machines. He personally looks after their maintenance, and has managed to get equipment that has been out of operation for years, working again.

In the past, our weavers brought their children to work, and it was only natural that they followed in their parents' footsteps. Today, however, the idea that weavers pass their knowledge on to their children, and that the children follow their parent's passion, no longer applies. Instead, Bevilacqua recruits artisans from art schools. They are trained for at least two years until they are allowed to use the loom. After five years, they can operate the loom on their own. In addition to finding the staff, finding suitable suppliers is a challenge these days. Tools for maintenance of the weaving machines, and good quality gold thread are also very hard to find.

DR MADDALENA VIANELLO
Marketing & Communications Manager

In 1937 Nino Barbantini was given the commission to refurbish the Teatro La Fenice in Venice. When it came to supplying the fabrics for the Sale Apollinee (the headquarters of the philharmonic society of the same name), and its antechambers, Tessitura Bevilaqua was chosen.

Everything was lost, however, when the Teatro La Fenice burned down in 1996 – architecture, furniture, furnishings, decorations and, of course, the upholstery, and wall coverings. The same fabrics could actually have been reproduced since Tessitura Bevilaqua had preserved the drawings and samples, as well as the old hand looms on which they were made. And there was a strong case for weaving them again, especially given that the principle underpinning the reconstruction was that everything was to be built "where and as it was". Unfortunately, the art of weaving does not enjoy the same kind of respect and appreciation as other applied arts rightly do. Similarly, given that most people believe that fabric can be replaced without respect for historical accuracy, it was decided to adopt simpler, alternative solutions.

• • •

The church of San Giuliano Martire was founded in the heart of Venice in 829. One fascinating item in the church is a vestment where the sumptuous pattern consists of a horizontal arrangement of a series of peacocks facing each other with the tree of life between them. Thanks to Bevilaqua weavers' professional skills, technical capacity and artistic flair, the originals are admirably reproduced in this vestment fabric. Considered generically as propitious in traditional iconography, the motif of birds (and especially paradisiacal birds like peacocks) facing each other with the tree of life between them appears not only in textiles but also in ceramics, metal objects, and jewellery. The motif of the peacock was to re-appear with various shades of meaning in early Christian iconography as a symbol of Christ in the tomb, on the grounds of the widely-held belief that his body was incorruptible. Similarly, the motif was an allusion to renewal and the resurrection because birds moult in spring.

• • •

On the transatlantic liner *Conte di Savoia*, launched at Trieste in October 1931, the grand Sala delle Feste (lounge) comes as a startling contrast in a series of rooms. The fabric used to upholster the furniture was figured "soprarizzo" velvet in the "giardino" pattern, produced by Bevilaqua. There was strong disagreement between traditionalists and advocates of the avant-garde, but it is surprising that no mention was made of the combination in the same room of sumptuous-looking furniture and new materials, such as linoleum, also widely used in the rest of the ship. It is even more surprising when we consider that the *Conte di Savoia* was a powerful lever of international propaganda for the fascist regime. In the early 1930s, Bevilaqua's contribution was meant to embody an Italian tradition, representing on the other side of the Atlantic an undying antique splendour still to be found in Italian industry under the regime. At the same time, traditional Italian industry was portrayed as being capable of working side by side with the production of new materials, the use of which the regime so ardently encouraged.

• • •

The phenomenon of revival, i.e. reference to styles from the past, is a constituent element in the fashion world. Examples go back as far as the Gothic period, and have continued right up to some striking cases in haute couture collections in recent years. Today, many leading international stylists follow this trend. Some interpret and experiment with earlier styles in a playful way, while others use them in designs for programmatic purposes. One particularly interesting example of this is the work of the leading Italian designers Domenico Dolce and Stefano Gabbana. At the start of their career, back in the early 1980s, they forged a signature style, in which sensuality and a predilection for a vaguely retro taste were fused to create an instantly recognisable, highly personal design label. For these two artists, the overall history of dress and fashion became an indispensable reference source. This programmatic strategy was a driving force in forging professional relations with Tessitura Bevilacqua.

Cantiere Navale
Camuffo

ITALY

For over 18 generations the oldest shipyard in the world has been famous for producing yachts known as "the Stradivari of the sea".

1438

The Camuffo shipyard at Portogruaro, which has been passed from father to son over eighteen successive generations of shipwrights, owners and expert foremen of all kinds of wooden boats, is regarded as the oldest shipyard in the world. Conclusive evidence of this is to be found in documents filed in the public archives of Pesaro, Rimini, Venice and Trieste, in Chioggia's archive and public library, as well as in the public diplomatic libraries, and historical maritime museums of Venice and Genoa Pegli.

Between the fifteenth and nineteenth centuries, the Camuffo yard built many different types of wooden boats for different uses: commerce, fishing or pleasure. After the Second World War, the family abandoned the construction of working vessels to concentrate exclusively on the production of pleasure boats.

Today

The Camuffo yachts are called the Stradivari del Mare (the Stradivari of the Sea).

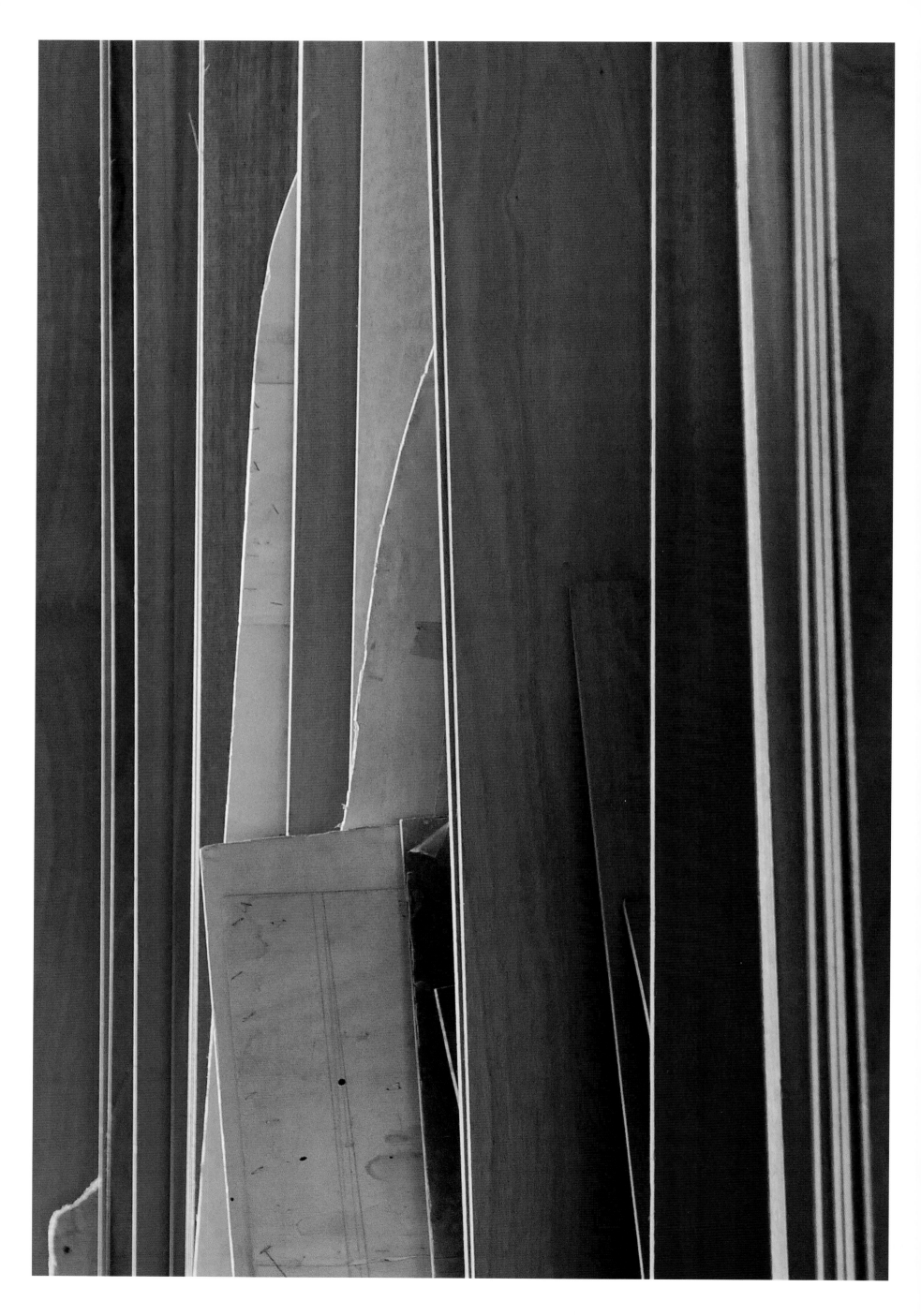

The yard's history goes back to 1438 in Candia, an important port on the Venetian island of the same name (now known as Crete), and the centre of all La Serenissima's trade from the Mediterranean towards the East and the Black Sea. The fortresses and arsenals of this Venetian duchy offered a safe refuge for Venice's trade convoys.

That year in Candia, a well-known foreman from the area called Camuffo, or El Ham-Mufti (meaning the foreman's voice in Arabic) was working for the Republic as a *magister stradii* — an expert tonnage measurer. Camuffo was responsible for establishing the carrying capacity of the various ships, which in turn determined the amount of tax to be paid to the State. Following the fall of Constantinople to the Ottomans, however, the situation in the Aegean Sea became a difficult one. For this reason, many inhabitants of the island moved to Chioggia, Italy, a centre for the construction of merchant vessels and fishing boats in the Adriatic.

• • •

The Camuffo family integrated well into the Venetian community, and established a successful boat-building business producing traditional sailing craft, fleets of working vessels for hire, and also locally introduced pleasure boating by hiring boats out for Sunday outings. The Camuffo family has guarded their construction methods, and precious secrets handed down over centuries of craft building, while also devising new technologies, such as the magical Camuffo hulls, the perfection of which has been recognised by all operators in the industry.

Progress with new types of adhesives led to a technological revolution for wood in the boat-building sector, resulting in the creation of different multi-layered plywoods. Wood treated chemically in this way is in fact capable of withstanding years of exposure to the elements, while maintaining its natural characteristics (elasticity, durability, and insulation); this makes it the very best material available for naval construction, and far superior to other materials such as fibreglass, steel, or aluminium. The plywoods are thoroughly dried before being worked, to ensure there are no internal tensions. In addition, the durability and flexibility of the material can be improved as necessary by varying the composition and thickness of the woods.

The Camuffo motor yachts are built from a tightly-knitted structure in solid wood worked closely with the grain so as to take advantage of the thread of the fibre, giving the main structure incomparable elasticity and dynamic absorption. This also allows for the formation of double bottoms and interspaces between the internal and external hulls, which, by recycling the air from below, creates a natural, constantly balanced, and condensation-free environment.

Carrara Marmo
ITALY

Known world over as the finest marble, the Carrara marble has made Carrara the stone centre of Europe.

50 BC

Carrara marble was used by the Romans from around 50 BC. According to Pliny the Elder, Caesar, in 48 BC, was the first to have a house built entirely of marble – both Carrara and Carystic.

16th Century

To regulate marble production, the Office of Marble was established in Carrara in 1564.

19th Century

Carrara was the unchallenged centre of stone processing during the nineteenth century, and the city prospered. There were many technical inventions in this period: for example in 1815, a stone-cutting saw with several blades for cutting natural stone that was powered by fast-moving water wheels, was invented in Carrara. Technology was continually improved, and eight iron frames were constructed, which made it possible for many large plates of marble only a centimetre thick to be produced. This process was exhibited at the world exhibition in Paris in 1867. In 1870, there were already over 80 sawmills of this kind in Carrara and the surrounding area.

20th Century

The beginning of the First World War was a disaster for Carrara's economy, as it brought marble production to a standstill. Production gradually recovered after the war but was halved by the global economic crisis in 1929. Mussolini's Fascist government tried to cope with the consequences of Italy's war with Ethiopia, and the sales losses resulting from it for Carrara marble, by commissioning monuments such as the building of the Forum Mussolini and the Mussolini Obelisk in Rome. These monumental commissions did little, however, to change Carrara's financial situation. The Second World War not only brought marble production to a halt, but also saw the destruction of most of the equipment in the stone quarries by the German army while it was fighting partisans from 1944 to 1945. Most of the population was involved in fierce resistance against the German occupiers. The anarcho-syndicalists, who had had a strong presence amongst the Carrara quarry workers since the nineteenth century, made Carrara a world centre of anarchism and played a major part in the resistance.

21st Century

Today, Carrara has to defend its status as the stone centre of Europe not only against Verona, a stone processing centre in the same country, but also against stone processing centres in China, India, and Brazil.

These quarries have been a provider of work for a whole region for centuries and have produced a legacy of masterpieces such as Michelangelo's David and the Pietà, the Campanile in Pisa and St Peters Basilica in Rome.

MAURO FRANCHINI
Quarry Worker

Michelangelo, Gian Lorenzo and Luigi Bernini, Pisano, Donatello, Canova, Rodin, Moore, César, Arp, and many other well-known sculptors have sourced their blocks of marble from the quarries in the Carrara mountains. The Renaissance sculptor Michelangelo helped to make the stone famous, carving the over five-metres tall David, the Pietà, Moses, and other sculptures from the material. Carrara marble has been used in the Florence Duomo, in the campanile in Pisa, in St Peter's in Rome, in the former World Trade Centre in New York, in casinos in Las Vegas, for the outer cladding of the Finlandia Hall in Helsinki, and for the Grande Arche de la Défense in Paris.

• • •

At the end of Italian romanticism, it became customary for sculptors to go to the Carrara mountains themselves to seek out their blocks of stone. These raw materials were transported to the exhibition venue, where they would be worked on. They were brought down into the valley by "lizzatura", a special method that was still in use to some extent up to the 1960s. The huge blocks would be secured with three hemp ropes (steel ropes were used from 1920 onwards), and the soaped-up wooden sledge would be transported to the valley by slackening the ropes, an extremely dangerous undertaking, which cost many lives.

In the valley, the raw materials were transported with a two-wheel (carrette) or four-wheel (currus) cart pulled by oxen. It was worked out that each pair of oxen could pull 800 kg on flat ground. Oxen pairs were used as a unit of measurement to calculate the costs of transport, and customs duties. In the course of industrialisation, the Carrara marble trade was facilitated by new financing concepts for the quarry owners. The oxen were replaced with steam traction engines. The infrastructure was considerably improved through the building of elevated cableways and railways for transporting stones into the valley as well as through the building of loading bridges in the harbour.

• • •

The employees came not only from Carrara but also from the surrounding villages. They had a long way to go to get to the quarries in the mountains. The quarry workers had to sleep in huts in the quarry during the week. Hard manual labour was the norm, and working conditions unsafe with long and unregulated working hours. Serious accidents were a frequent occurrence. These led to industrial disputes, in response to which, among other things, children's homes and poorhouses were built, public-care institutions were founded, and a vocational school established.

• • •

Besides being used in sculpture and monuments, Carrara marble has many further applications in interior and exterior fittings. Worktables made of Carrara marble are often found in the confectionery business, as icing must cool quickly, and marble surfaces are particularly well-suited to ensuring this. Another consideration is that dough does not stick to the marble surfaces. One characteristic has led to a gourmet speciality: the *lardo di Colonnata* (bacon from Colonnata) is a very fatty bacon, which is placed in purpose-made marble troughs with salt, spices and herbs, and left to mature for at least six months. Lardo di Colonnata used to be the food of quarry workers, who needed nourishment that was high in calories for their hard work. As in other marble extraction sites, half-blocks of marble that were not going to be put to economic use were ground up into a powder with pieces the size of a thousandth of a millimetre, which was used in toothpaste, soap, scouring agents, and also in glass and paper production. Recently, a marble piano with innards by Steinway was produced for the rock band Bon Jovi. The instrument made its debut at a concert held inside an obsolete marble quarry in Carrara. It has since been played by Elton John, Lang Lang, and Andrea Bocelli.

• • •

For centuries generations earned their living in the quarries of Carrara and the surrounding area. Typical of all of them is this account of a working life: Mauro Franchini was a quarry worker and a true craftsman. The economic situation meant that he had to seek work all over the world, including in Africa, Albania, Arabia, and Asia. He joined the anarchist partisan groups at a young age during the Second World War. In 1945, he was one of the founders of the Federazione Anarchia Italiana (FAI), and he was involved in many anarchist initiatives in the area. He was one of those who reconstructed the marble bridge at Carrara after the Fascists had demolished it with explosives in 1945. He was also instrumental in the establishment of the local monument to the victims of Fascism, and was involved in many rallies, debates, and public meetings. In the last year of his life, he was very ill but continued to take part in anarchist activities as much as he could.

Benediktiner Kloster Disentis

SWITZERLAND

*Almost 1,300 years old, the monastery is an impressive example
of survival under difficult circumstances, and continues to be
an important economic factor for the region.*

c. 720 AD

Disentis Monastery is an abbey of the Swiss Benedictine congregation in the Canton of Graubünden, where the Lukmanier and Oberalp passes meet. The abbey was founded in 720 by the wandering Frankish monk Sigisbert with the help of a local magnate called Placidus. It is named in honour of St Martin; the building we see today dates from the late seventeenth century.

As a spiritual place, the monastery is open to visitors looking to discover or deepen their faith; it also hosts conferences, cultural events and seminars. The community of twenty-eight monks employs a staff of seventy with a range of professional skills. In addition to the monastic life, an important activity is running the monastery school. Thanks to the monastery, it is possible to have a secondary school education in the isolated valley of Surselva. The addition of a boarding school for girls is a sign of how the monastery forms a living bridge between tradition and modernity. Another symbol is the chapel of Caplutta Sogn Benedetg at Sumvitg, built by Peter Zumthor in 1989, which also belongs to the monastery.

Business is very important for running and developing the monastery: a master plan is used as a strategic management tool. The monastery is an important economic factor for the region.

BENEDIKTINER
KLOSTER DISENTIS

Dringend notwendig:

Restauri
Kl

How can each individual and the community continue to develop here in this place as circumstances constantly change? Stability demands that we consciously face up to the signs of the times. This is the only way we can be of service to the church and society today. It is also the only way we find a path into the future. The monastic community has to constantly engage itself in and alongside this world. That requires the courage to try out new things, and to make change happen. This constant stepping forward, however, also needs fixed points and constants: stabilitas in progressu.

ABBOT VIGELI MONN

Sixty-sixth Abbot of Disentis Monastery

We do not know exactly when the Frankish monk Sigisbert settled in Disentis. He was joined by Placidus, an important local landowner. The ruler of the region, Victor of Chur, felt that his privileges were under threat, however, and had Placidus murdered.

The first documentary mention of the monastery was in 765 in the will of Tello, Bishop of Chur. In 940 the monastery was destroyed by marauding Saracens. The monks fled but returned to rebuild it. During the Reformation, in the fifteenth and sixteenth centuries, the monastery reached a low point in its history: burned down several times, the buildings collapsed. Famine, plague, and the persecution of witches stalked the land. Gradually, a religious and spiritual revival led to the construction of new baroque buildings in 1685, and to consecration of the church in 1712. The monastery today is a monumental construction that stands worthy of comparison to the palaces of the Italian renaissance and the early baroque.

Towards the end of the French Revolution, in spring 1799, French troops plundered the monastery. On 1 May 1799 the local people revolted against the French army. The abbey and village were set on fire on 6 May, in reprisal. Having already lost the Benedictine estates in the Veltlin, all that was left was "rubble and debts". Reconstruction moved ahead slowly until another fire in 1846 caused a setback. Worse, the cantonal authorities placed the monastery under state control: the cantonal Monastery Act of 1861 made it almost impossible to take on novices. Reduced to poverty, the monastery community faced total collapse. A rethink began in 1880, as the mood changed among the people and in government. With assistance from the Swiss Benedictine congregation, the monastery was saved from collapse and blossomed anew in the twentieth century.

• • •

A new CODEX as described below, was adopted at the beginning of the twenty-first century: the behavioural guidelines apply to everyone, regardless of whether they be monk or employee.

ORA – the ability to feel

- First comes respect for creation and the human individual.
- Out of respect for personal dignity, I stay close or distant as appropriate.
- I act appropriately in my dealings with others – as regards the place, the nature of the other person, the context of our meeting, and my choice of clothing.
- I behave reliably and considerately, and reflect on my conduct. I remain open to the responses of others.
- I take care of my physical and spiritual wellbeing, and respect these values with my neighbour.

LEGE – the ability to relate

- I encourage myself and my neighbour to develop our own positions as we engage with our own values, and with those of the Benedictine community in the monastery.
- I take strength from concern for my wellbeing, and my contributions to the community.
- When using digital media, I am attentive to the forms and dangers of what I communicate.

LABORA – the ability to work

- My interest, curiosity and questions are explicitly solicited; they also demonstrate my willingness to constructively support development.
- I ask for support when I need it, and I give support whenever I can.
- As I journey on my life path I set an example for others in my striving for quality and reliability.

• • •

The senior Abbot summarized the philosophy of the monastery as follows: *Stabilitas in progressu* – striking the balance between stability and progress – is one of the challenges the monastery faces. Benedictines prize stability along with obedience and the monastic life. That means stability in place, and in the community. The most important constants in the Benedictine life lie in the regular alternation of prayer, reading, and work. The rhythm this gives to monastic life is crucial. It provides a reference point and meaning for each individual, and for the community. Key fixed points are reflected in the values the monastic community follows: values such as respect for our fellow human beings, their talents and weaknesses, tender care for the old and the sick, treating the monastic property and possessions carefully, and being modest in one's own needs and requests.

The East India Company
UK

Granted a Royal Charter in 1600, the company had a monopoly on all trade between Britain and Asia, and is today a merchandiser of select luxury goods.

1600

Granted a Royal Charter by Queen Elizabeth I, the East India Company was formed to engage in trade with East and South-East Asia and India. The Company was established with 125 shareholders and £72,000 in capital; its corporate structure was the earliest example of a joint stock company. Starting as a monopolistic trading body, the Company became involved in politics and acted as an agent of British imperialism in India from the early eighteenth century to the mid-nineteenth century.

As the Company grew, it mapped trade routes through unchartered territory, and changed social customs, tastes, and ways of thought to influence the very fabric of our lives today. Motivated by a pioneering spirit and sense of adventure, the Company created British India, founded Hong Kong and Singapore, was the cause of the Boston Tea Party, employed Captain Kidd to combat piracy, and held Napoleon captive. At one point, the Company conducted and controlled 50 per cent of world trade. Tea accounted for more than 60 per cent of the Company's total trade in the late eighteenth century.

Their warehouses were places of wonder, stocking silks, chintzes, calicos, porcelain, coffees, chocolates, and spices from around the world that people had never seen before. The Company introduced tea to Britain and India, woollens to Japan, chintzes to America, spices to the West Indies, opium to China, porcelain to Russia, and polo to Persia. It had its own armies, navies, currencies, and territories as diverse as the tiny Spice Island, Pulo Run (later exchanged for Manhattan), and the Jewel in the Crown, India itself. As the *Times* newspaper reported in 1874 when the Company was finally absorbed by the Crown: "It is just as well to record that it accomplished a work such as in the whole history of the human race no other Company ever attempted and, as such, is ever likely to attempt in the years to come."

Royal Bone China
Benjarong
18ct Gold

The world is one of colour, of opportunity, of diversity, of beauty. But in today's seemingly connected society, it's all too easy to forget this, and to accept the uniformity and monotony that is offered to us. We believe the world needs vibrancy, indulgence, and inspiration. We believe people should never stop discovering, never stop being surprised. Having remarkable connections, we see our role as bringing together the best our world has to offer — to create unique goods that help people to explore and experience what's out there. Products that help people see their world in a different and better light. Products that have the power to amaze and astonish.

SANJIV M. MEHTA
Chairman and Managing Director

Sanjiv Mehta, the Indian owner, bought the East India Company from its thirty or forty owners with a fifteen-million-dollar investment in 2005. He did not take this step lightly: "Put yourself in my shoes for a moment. On a rational plane, when I bought the Company, I saw gold at the end of the rainbow. But, at an emotional level, as an Indian, when you think with your heart as I do, I had this huge feeling of redemption — this indescribable feeling of owning a company that once owned us." When Mehta took over, his objective was to understand its history. He took a sabbatical from all other business, and travelled around the world, visiting former East India Company trading posts and museums, reading records, and meeting people who understood the business of that time.

• • •

The Company delivers no ordinary products — it means every one of them is imbued with a special quality. An element that adds a touch of luxury, a taste of the exotic, a sense of intrigue, or that simply adds richness to a world where this was previously lacking.

It could be an ingredient in a recipe; it could be a material that was used. It could be the place where the Company sourced the material, or the skill of the craftsman who created it. Whatever it is, it's something that's special, a fusion of influences that's unique to the East India Company.

• • •

The Company had a monopoly on all trade to Britain from the East and, although it was originally set up to trade spices, it quickly found that there were many other products from the Orient, such as tea, that could find a ready market back home.

Brought by the Company as a gift for King Charles II, tea leaves were passed on to his wife, Queen Catherine of Braganza, who had grown up with tea in her native Portugal. She then slowly introduced this curious drink into aristocratic and noble circles, beginning a tradition that would last for centuries. Initially, tea leaves arrived in small quantities, and were so expensive, that only the upper class could afford them. Later, the Company introduced the fashion of adding sugar to tea, leading to more frequent consumption of tea, and a rise in the import of sugar.

• • •

Europeans quickly became accustomed to the richly spiced foods of India through banquets given by Indian princes for their European counterparts. In the late eighteenth century, the Company began to experiment with planting spices from one country in another, using its network of Botanical Gardens to propagate the seeds. This is why, pepper, cloves, nutmeg and cinnamon can be found in the West Indies today, where they have helped create the distinctive Cajun cuisine.

• • •

The East India Company was aware that coffee was an important trading commodity in the East, and as early as 1607 had sent ships to visit Aden and adjacent ports to explore the possibilities. Rather than bringing it back to Europe, where there was as yet little demand for coffee, the Company started selling it in Persia and Mughal India. Once the coffee house boom started at the end of the seventeenth century, however, the Company became the largest and most successful importer for the British market.

• • •

After 1650, chocolate began to be sold in all the principal cities of Europe, first in the then burgeoning coffee houses, and later in dedicated chocolate shops. To service a rapid increase in popularity, chocolate pots and cups of silver or porcelain were soon being made all over Europe.

Needless to say, the governments of the day seized upon the import of chocolate as a potential source of revenue, and high taxes were imposed. By the time of the reign of George III, the Company had to pay two shillings in tax per pound of cocoa imported into Britain.

• • •

We're pioneers, inventors, explorers and dreamers.
We're honourable merchants.
We're the East India Company.
Reborn and renewed.
A company re-invented for today.

Faber-Castell
GERMANY

The first global manufacturer of wooden pencils, this family-owned firm is today one of the most important producers of sophisticated writing instruments in the world.

1761

The first documentary evidence of pencil makers dates back to Nuremberg in 1660. A number of workshops were established in the surrounding countryside, and in particular in the small town of Stein. There, the carpenter Kaspar Faber set himself up in business with his own workshop in 1761, and was so successful at making pencils that he was able to hand quite a respectable business on to his son.

Today

Faber-Castell is one of the oldest family-owned industrial firms in the world, now in the hands of its eighth generation. The business operates in over 120 countries. Faber-Castell has factories in nine countries, and distribution companies in twenty-three countries worldwide.

With more than two billion lead and coloured pencils produced every year, Faber-Castell is the most globally significant manufacturer of wooden pencils. The company has its traditional commitment to high quality, and a great number of product innovations to thank for its leading position in the international market.

Faber-Castell's portfolio consists of five areas of expertise: Playing and learning, art and graphics, premium, general writing, and marking as well as cosmetics.

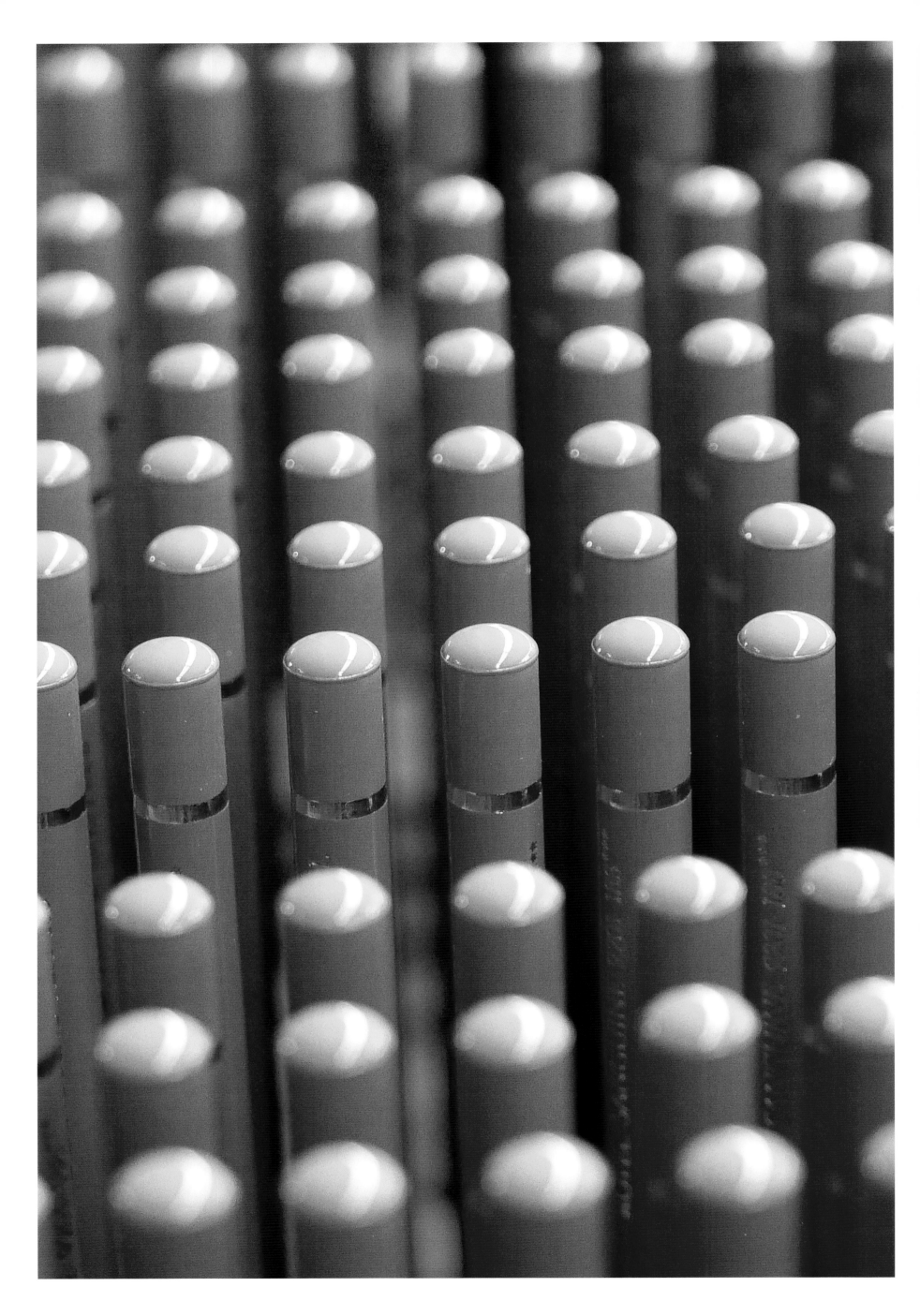

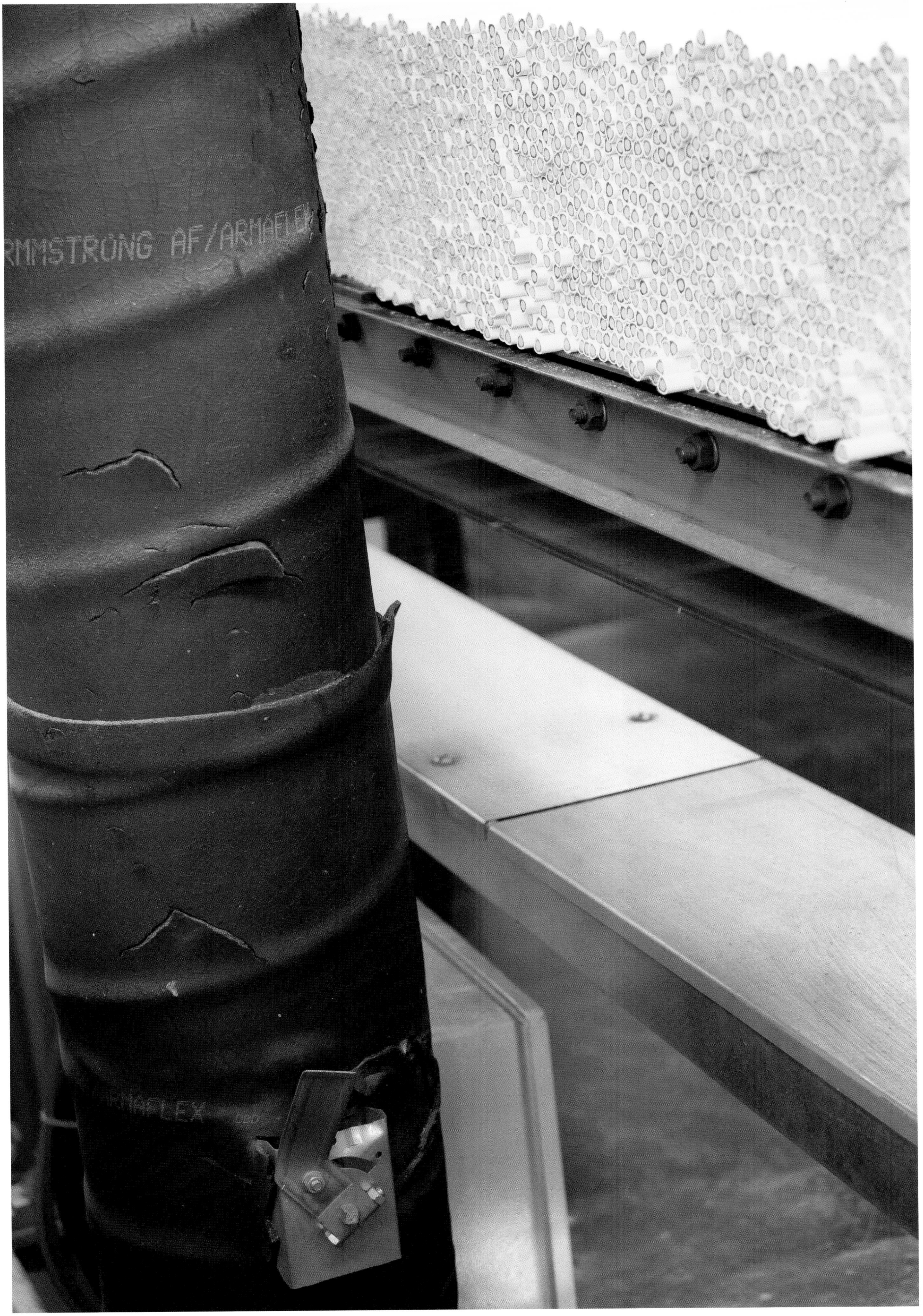
RMMSTRONG AF/ARMAFLEX
RMAFLEX

It is important to be passionate about customer needs, meeting them and being faithful to our motto: the highest priority for the future of the company is to make ordinary things extraordinarily good.

ANTON-WOLFGANG COUNT VON FABER-CASTELL
Eighth Generation

At the beginning of the sixteenth century, a black shiny material was discovered in the English county of Cumberland, which was used as the predecessor of today's pencils. It was believed to be lead ore. It was not until the end of the eighteenth century that it was identified to be, like diamonds, pure carbon. The material was named graphite, derived from the Greek "graphein" (to write). Starting in the nineteenth century, clay and graphite were mixed to produce pencil leads in different degrees of hardness. Though misleading, "lead" pencils do not actually contain lead at all.

• • •

An important pioneer in the history of the company was Baron Lothar von Faber. He took over the pencil factory in 1839, and succeeded in producing pencils of outstanding quality: "From the very start, my sole concern was to become the best, by making the best to be made anywhere in the world". He labelled the pencils with the company name A.W. Faber, and in doing so, developed the first brand pencil in the world. With the filing of a petition for protection from the numerous fakes made by competitors, the company became a pioneer in trademark protection laws.

Lothar von Faber thought globally from the very beginning, and founded a branch in the New World – New York. This was followed by trading houses in London, Paris, Vienna, and St. Petersburg. In a brilliant tactical move, Lothar von Faber secured the sole rights to a graphite mine in Siberia in 1856, which at the time produced the best graphite in the world.

He also proved himself a responsible entrepreneur. His social institutions included the first company health insurance fund, and one of the first kindergartens in Germany, as well as schools and accommodation for workers, which were seen as so exemplary that even the French emperor Napoleon III sent an expert delegation to Stein to investigate.

• • •

Artists and other creative people through the ages have placed their trust in the Faber-Castell brand name. That's why there are quotes from figures such as Alexander Solzhenitsyn, Günther Grass, Vladimir Nabokov and Karl Lagerfeld, testifying to a love for the company's products, not to mention what Vincent van Gogh wrote in a letter to his friend Anthon van Rappard in 1883: "I also wanted to tell you about a sort of pencil by Faber which I have found. They are of this thickness, rather soft and better quality than the Zimmermann pencil, are splendidly black, and you can work very comfortably with them for long studies."

• • •

The advertising motif of the two fighting pencil knights was created especially for the top product CASTELL 9000 in 1905. Seen as less than contemporary, it disappeared from view for a while. From the beginning of the 1990s, the company reformulated its corporate design. The knight motif was reborn as the trademark, and today it is part of the company logo in stylised form.

• • •

Pencils are nowadays produced in almost completely automatic "pencil streets". These so-called raw pencil machines assemble the pencils from leads and wooden planks. The main elements of the leads are graphite and clay. The graphite gives them their black colour, and the clay serves as a binding agent, giving them shape and solidity. Both are mixed for different degrees of hardness and this mixture is pressed through a nozzle into lead sticks under high pressure. The lead sticks are cut to pencil length while still soft, then fired once dry, and dipped into an oil bath, to achieve a smooth line. Afterwards, they are encased in wood. For this, wooden logs are cut into small planks. They must be stored for several months, until they are completely dry. Only at this point will they be shaped into flutes for the lead. After the leads have been inserted, a second plank is placed, glued, and pressed. Afterwards, the planing machine strips the pencil-blanks. They are then coated several times in a water-based varnish, stamped, dipped (for the end cap), and lastly sharpened.

• • •

As a forerunner in the industry for environment-friendly industrial assembly processes, Faber-Castell has owned their most important resource, wood, from the mid-1980s. The company works with a quick-growing coniferous wood from its own forest in Brazil and maintains nurseries. Under a reforestation scheme, harvested rows of trees are constantly replanted. On a total surface area of about 10,000 hectares, 1000 kilometres away from the Amazonian rainforest, over one million seedlings of the genus Pinus Caribea are planted and reared every year. In just ten to twelve years, they are tall enough to be harvested. Pencils are produced using these environment-friendly resources.

Farina
Eau de Cologne
GERMANY

The oldest continuously-operating perfume manufacturer in the world has developed the model for a whole class of fragrances.

1709

More than 300 years ago, the oldest continuously operating perfume factory in the world, Johann Maria Farina gegenüber dem Jülichs-Platz, was founded in Cologne. The perfumer Johann Maria Farina (1686-1766) arrived in Cologne from Italy; he named his perfume Eau de Cologne in honour of his adopted city. In doing so, he made Cologne famous for its perfume. The city honoured its citizen with a statue on the council tower. The perfumer Johann Maria Farina brought knowledge of how to distil pure alcohol from Italy. This was the foundation of his successful creation, and he wrote: "My perfume is like an Italian spring morning after the rain, oranges, grapefruit, lemons, bergamot, cedar, lime, and the petals and herbs of my homeland. It refreshes me, awakens my senses and imagination."

European royal families adored the perfume, granting Farina over fifty royal purveyor titles. When Eau de Cologne was mentioned in the eighteenth century, it always referred to Farina's perfume. The success meant that a whole class of perfume was born from the name. Today the original Eau de Cologne is produced by the eighth generation of the Farina family.

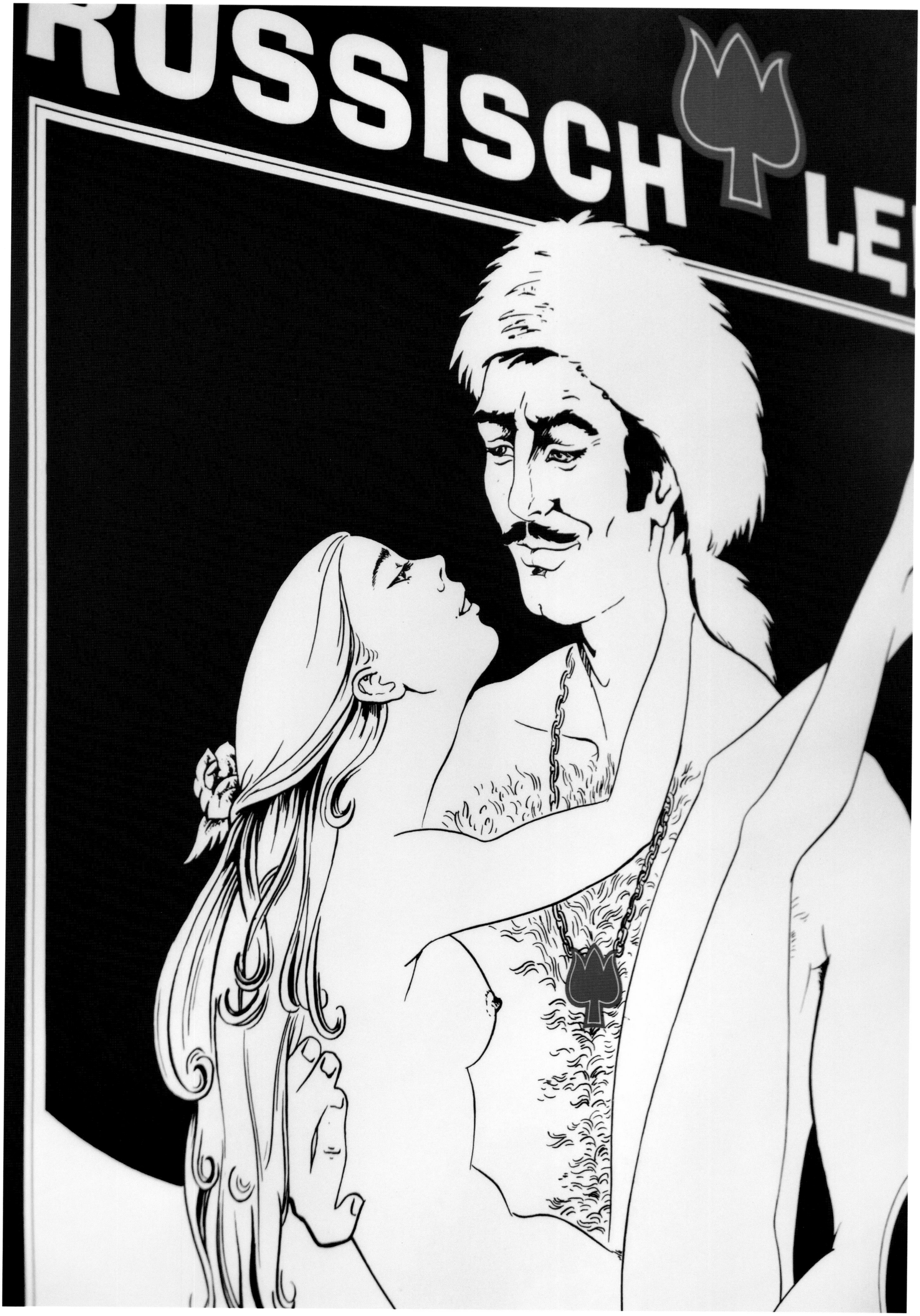
RUSSISCH

Our guiding principle is to maintain that which has been preserved.

JOHANN MARIA FARINA
Managing Director

Who hasn't sensed it? A single touch wafting over us as we enter a house, the trace of perfume that floats around us when a stranger walks past – and another world is opened up. With all our senses, we apprehend what one sniff has communicated to us. Hardly anything is so much a gift to us as our sense of smell. Who sees, sees. Who hears, hears. Who feels for something or tastes something, seizes and enjoys. We carefully attune our sense of hearing or sight to our feelings or to what we find attractive. But the sense of smell is a higher art. It is the sense most strongly associated with memory, the complex archive of our soul's stirrings.

• • •

Seventeenth-century Italian flavourists already knew how to distil pure alcohol from quality wine. Only in alcohol can the essences of petals, fruits or balsamic extracts be satisfactorily dissolved. Only alcohol can offer the pure unaltered aroma of the extracts to the olfactory nerves. It doesn't mix body odour and perfume aroma, but masks the smell of the wearer. It was, and is, the only way to fleetingly recall and transmit each perfume. Johann Maria Farina perfectly mastered the art of distillation, and brought ever more extracts in combination with the pure spirit of the wine.

• • •

There was a major boom for the Eau de Cologne trade during the Seven Years' War. Farina supplied officers from both French Rhine armies, for whom the perfume had become an intrinsic part of their equipment along with wigs, powder, and other luxury items. The French officers in turn sent the Eau de Cologne to their wives, friends and girlfriends at home.

• • •

For Johann Maria, the purity and quality of the extracts used were most important. If he didn't like the extracts delivered to him, he imported the whole fruits, and distilled them himself. In terms of logistics, that entailed an enormous amount of effort. How was fruit supposed to survive the week-long journey, and remain not only unharmed, but also fresh?

• • •

Johann Maria's Eau de Cologne, the Italian spring morning, was not concocted in a laboratory, but first and foremost in his mind. Like a conductor with a musical score, he envisioned the invented and undisclosed notes of the future sound of his extracts' not-yet played symphony. Even before he actually smelled the swelling sequence of chords and sounded out the melody, he left dozens of extracts to express themselves in his mind, both in unison and polyphonically. This capacity for imagination is what makes a perfect sense of smell such an asset.

• • •

Johann Maria wanted this symphony of fragrances to always sound the same, and hence be unmistakeable. Three hundred years ago, a project of this kind was stunningly new, as citrus bergamia produces fruits with differing aromatic notes depending on the year and the weather conditions. The quality of the soil may mean that one grapefruit tree is not one and the same thing as another.

Today it is taken for granted that a perfume always smells the same. If, though, you want to work with natural aromas, which Farina continues to do as far as possible, then the very best extracts must be recreated every year. Johann Maria took samples of every extract and mixture for this purpose, which still exist. In doing so, he wanted to preserve the particular qualities of each year's harvest.

• • •

Every delivery included a printed information sheet signed by Farina. According to these instructions, the water was not only to be used for outer application, but could also be used to care for the teeth, and to fend off contagious diseases.

Until the nineteenth century, Farina exported the perfume in green oblong blown-glass bottles, named "rosolios". Extremely expensive to produce, these coloured bottles were sealed with a cork, and also protected their contents from light to prevent deterioration in quality. At first the perfume was filled into small porcelain jugs for use. But no later than 1836, with the introduction of the first self-standing bottles, the packaging became an important guarantee of its success. From then on, it was subject to the changing tastes and fashions of the day, as pragmatism gave way to design.

Caffé Florian
ITALY

As the oldest coffeehouse in continuous operation, this establishment has hosted many famous names from the worlds of literature, music, films and politics.

1720

In 1720 Floriano Francesconi opened a coffeehouse under the arcades of Procuratie Nuove, and gave it the name 'Alla Venezia Trionfante', or Triumphant Venice. One of many coffeehouses in Venice, the establishment quickly – perhaps because of its owner's outgoing character and flamboyant personality – became very popular with intellectuals, artists, and noblemen, who soon took to calling it Florian's. The name stuck, and even today everyone calls it by that name. Little did the owner know that what was at first no more than two simply furnished rooms would become the oldest coffeehouse in continuous operation.

1858

In the mid-nineteenth century, the Caffé Florian changed ownership and the architect Ludovico Cadorin was commissioned to carry out an extensive renovation of the enlarged Florian interiors, creating the ornate splendour that can still be admired today. At the time, the restoration prompted a great public outcry because of the opulence of the furniture, mirrors, paintings, gilded friezes, and cornices.

Today

Today, Caffé Florian belongs to the Fendi family, renowned art collectors and formerly, owners of the fashion house of the same name. The Florian style has now spread beyond the boundaries of the lagoon city with the opening of cafés bearing the same name in Florence and Rome as well as in London, Dubai, and Suzhou.

The Turks, it was said, adored coffee, both in their own country, and in Egypt. The Venetian government was at first wary, and carefully scrutinised reports from its ambassadors; it waited for some time before allowing this plant with its medicinal properties to take root in the city. Why such delay? The Venetian authorities were uneasy. Disturbing rumours had been filtering in from Istanbul, where it was said that coffee had been wreaking havoc on several fronts. Excessive consumption was apparently inciting women to lascivious behaviour that, despite being considered unseemly, would have been forgivable in the eyes of many Venetians. However, its reputed effects on men were more serious: loss of virility, a weakening of the character, an inclination towards the exclusive company of men, and sodomy; eloquent proof of this could be found at a number of cafés and public baths. Venice could not afford to risk such an assault on moral standards. It was one thing for women to seek out their own pleasures in a city which had since the sixteenth century been publishing a detailed guide to the most sought-after local courtesans. As for the men, who held such power in their hands, the Republic could not possibly permit them to follow the same twisted path as the Turks: the "Oriental vice" of homosexuality was already popular enough in the city!

• • •

The first Venetian magazine, the *Gazzetta Veneta*, was born at the Florian in 1760, at the instigation of Count Gasparo Gozzi, who spent many hours in the cafés watching customers, and listening to them talk. He noted that while Venetians might be interested in world events, they were still more curious about the great and small goings-on in their own city. The *Gazzetta Veneta* offered detailed reports of local events and the latest society news and gossip, and supplied useful information about public occasions, books, business and trade, not to mention a small advertising section.

• • •

In 1776, the Council of Ten took one of the most unpopular decisions in Venetian history: women were prohibited from entering cafés, either by day or by night, once the carnival had ended. The official reason for this ban was that games of chance were being played in the cafés, but more important was that there was a proliferation of courtesans in these establishments. It was a hypocritical decree, for the courtesans were wily, and continued to flaunt their wares dressed as doges' wives. The owner of Caffé Florian, however, appealed to the State Inquisitors, and explained that there was a small room which could be accessed by a route other than the main entrance. Would it be possible for him to receive "a number of my very dear clients, honest subjects, accompanied by their own wives, as well as other ladies from their families?" The Inquisitors relented, and granted permission for ladies to be received at the Florian.

• • •

Leafing through the Florian guestbook since the 1930s, one finds many famous names from the world of literature, music, films and politics: Arthur Rubinstein, Richard Strauss, Ernest Hemingway, Marcello Mastroianni, Giorgio De Chirico, Anthony Quinn, Princess Grace of Monaco, Jean-Paul Sartre, Liza Minnelli, Queen Elizabeth and the Queen Mother, François Mitterrand, Margaret Thatcher, Jacques Chirac, Helmut Kohl… and the list goes on… It would be the same trying to name all the films made in Venice in which the protagonists meet at the Florian.
Luckily, the cosmopolitan frenzy does nothing to stop the Venetians themselves from frequenting their own café. And, logically speaking, if so many famous people come here to pledge their allegiance to the Caffé Florian, surely that demonstrates that the café itself is just as important as they are, if not more so… *non è vero?*

• • •

It was in 1893, in the Florian, that the idea for the International Exhibition of Art of the City of Venice, soon to be known as the Venice Biennale of modern art, was born. The Biennale was an unqualified success. This has led to the establishment of several artistic events: since the 1980s, every two years, at the Temporanea – the Art of the Possible at the Caffé Florian, an exhibition linked to the Biennale – an artist is invited to set up a display in one room or another of the café. At the same time, Unica, a contemporary work of art for the Florian, allows an artist to create a single piece inspired by the location. However, the two main exhibitions do not prevent the café from presenting more focused events during the course of the seasons. In making the choice of opening the establishment to artistic shows, the pitfall of letting the Florian become a museum has been avoided, as are so many places nowadays in Venice.

Hand & Lock,
Embroidery
UK

The embroidery house has created masterpieces for the Queen, the Queen Mother, and Princess Diana, and continues to produce specialist textiles for blockbuster movies and the London Fashion Week.

1767

Hand & Lock is an embroidery brand created from a fusion of two long established embroidery businesses – M. Hand and S. Lock.

In 1767 a Huguenot refugee known as M. Hand added embroidery to his range of laces, and set up M. Hand & Co.

1898

In 1898, C. E. Phipps & Co. opened an embroidery business supporting the burgeoning London couture fashion houses. By 1956 it had survived the wars as a modest but well-established business when Mr Phipps retired, and a young designer, Stanley Lock, took over from him. The company was renamed S. Lock Ltd., and reached new heights. Taking notice of S. Lock's success, the monarchy awarded the firm a Royal Warrant. Royal commissions have included gowns for the Queen, the Queen Mother, and Princess Anne's wedding ensemble. Princess Diana added new glamour with her love of richly embroidered garments.

2001

In 2001, the two companies M. Hand and S. Lock merged, and the Hand & Lock brand was created.

As a traditional embroidery company, our heritage goes back to Roman times, and we have become world-renowned as providers of the finest hand embroidery. We are a living antique, but moving with the times, bringing hand embroidery into the present. We are ready to take on all types of embroidery, big and small, and our rich history guarantees our clients consistency and quality every time.

ALASTAIR MACLEOD
Chairman

Good tailoring without embroidery is like a blank canvas without paint or a blue sky without clouds. Embellishment offers colour, drama, sunsets, and accent. Embroidery is the jazz singer that accompanies the band. For thousands of years, decorative patterns have been stitched into the most humble garments, and over time the techniques used have developed into sophisticated art forms.

• • •

The Hand & Lock archive reveals the intriguing history of the company, from forgotten designer collaborations to military embroidery sketches from the nineteenth century and earlier. So when Hand & Lock opened a brown folder containing three delicate envelopes addressed to Mr Lock postmarked 1947, along with a few photographic prints, quite a special part of the company's past was uncovered: "Thank you so much for the wonderful embroidery you have done on Paulette Goddard's dress", begins the first letter signed by Cecil Beaton, one of the most inspirational fashion photographers of the twentieth century.

• • •

Contemporary artist Jake Chapman is the art curator for Peace One Day and asked artists to produce art from decommissioned M16 assault rifles. Hand & Lock was approached with the idea of a fully embroidered rifle wrought in goldwork. The rifle arrived at the studio, and caused a commotion when it was unwrapped. Under the many layers of bubble wrap lay the dark steel and aluminium rifle presenting the team with an unusual challenge. But, slowly the steel was covered with cloth of silver and the hard edges and details were embellished in gold and black bullions. The completed gun joined others made by Damien Hirst, Sarah Lucas and Sam Taylor-Johnson, and was auctioned to raise funds for charity.

• • •

When it comes to military embroidery, the range of products includes tassels, shoulder cords, epaulettes, aiguillettes, gorgets, sword knots, and netted buttons. Hand & Lock also offers a bespoke range of products for the British Army, Royal Navy and Royal Air Force, as well as for the American, Canadian, and Mexican armed forces. Drafts for rare badges and emblems dating back to the 1700s exist in the archive, and are often retrieved to make new designs. Designs in the archive that incorporate royal crowns have to be updated to the present monarch and their chosen crown. Along with the crown, the cypher might have to be changed. A big part of the day-to-day work, this has changed little over 250 years. The team of designers still takes delicate drafts laid out on tracing paper, and redraws them with updates and changes. The designer adds annotations detailing the direction of stitch, the height of 'relief', and the exact colours to be used for the embroiderers to work from. Working entirely by hand, they painstakingly lay each coil of bullion to bring the design to life. The process cannot be replicated by machine, and remains a rare and difficult skill requiring patience and an exceptional attention to detail.

• • •

Embroidery is the antithesis of mass production; each piece a labour of love, and one of a kind. Hand & Lock's embroiderers, all in their twenties, have stitched pieces for clients such as Liberty, Hermès, Kate Moss, Rihanna, Adidas, Nike, Tom Ford, Louis Vuitton, and Chanel.

• • •

The idea of producing a Hand & Lock collection for London Fashion Week first came up in a staff meeting. The feeling was that the time was right for Hand & Lock to produce pieces to highlight its skills and expertise. A brief was written factoring in elements of Hand & Lock military heritage, and then inverted with ideas of rebellion and jungle law. The lion-face jumper signifies self-empowerment; the lion has long been a symbol of inner strength. Constructed meticulously from metal and feathers, the fully sequined tracksuit draws inspiration from military jackets and tiger stripes; a uniform of protest, it represents the strength and power of the dispossessed.

• • •

Hand & Lock initiated the prestigious embroidery prize at the beginning of the twenty-first century. The Prize is an invaluable opportunity for new designers to showcase their finest creations. The submissions have to showcase design skills as well as the ability to embroider by hand. The object can be a piece of fashion, a piece of jewellery, an artistic sculpture, an embroidered tapestry, a piece for home interior design, etc. The judges look at the concept, execution, embroidery skill, and overall presentation.

The Eternal Mewar

INDIA

A unique heritage brand exemplifying hospitality, cultural preservation, education and sports for global audiences. Acknowledged as the world's oldest serving dynasty.

734

Intangible ideas need tangible expression; it was an idea whose time had come.

In 2006 Eternal Mewar was created to provide a tangible expression of the House of Mewar. Acknowledged as the world's oldest-serving dynasty, the House of Mewar, with a "Rana" or "Maharana" at the helm, has faced political turmoil, foreign invasions, colonial rule, and socio-economic upheavals over the past 1,400 years. These challenges tested the commitment of the House to adhere to the "Custodianship form of governance": a unique value-system received in trust from Guru Harit Rashi by the founding father of the House, Bappa Rawal, in 734 AD.

Every generation of the Maharanas — to date, seventy-six generations — has served not as rulers or owners, but as Custodians or Trustees of the tangible and intangible legacies they inherited. In each era, they upheld the five values of honour — self-reliance, independence, service to, and respect for all humanity.

Eternal Mewar — which is explicated with the words *Custodianship Unbroken Since 734 AD,* encompasses these core values and the legacy of the House. It covers all initiatives of the House of Mewar, which bridge the historic past with an unpredictable future.

1993

Shriji Arvind Singh Mewar, the present Custodian, began a soul-searching journey in 1993 with the publication of *Inheritance 76*, a document outlining the opportunities and threats he perceived as the seventy-sixth Custodian. Eternal Mewar is a confluence of his thoughts and actions. In 2014 he said, "*Inheritance 76* is our 'road map' for the sustainability and longevity of the family, its values, and its business."

Today

In the age of globalisation, Eternal Mewar is no longer just an established heritage brand but essentially a vibrant catalyst, which continues to sustain the living heritage of Mewar, and the civilisational ethos of India. In everything Eternal Mewar does, it exemplifies hospitality, cultural preservation, education, philanthropy, sports, and spirituality for global and Indian audiences.

Building cities, sustaining tomorrows:

It was hailed as the mightiest fort of its time: the impregnable fort-city named Chittorgarh in the heart of arid south Rajasthan. From the eighth to sixteenth centuries, Chittorgarh was the capital of the Kingdom of Mewar, complete with towering walls stretching for miles, moats, palaces and temples, homes and granaries that sustained generations of Ranas, their clans and the citizens they protected. What each generation built, provided a livelihood for thousands through the patronage of architects, sculptors, artists, and artisans from all over the region. The Ranas practised in the tenth to thirteenth centuries, the Keynesian economics of the modern twentieth: Initiating city-development projects for public welfare for generations.

Like Pompeii in Greece, Chittorgarh may lie in ruins today but the impact of the achievements of the Ranas has survived in Rajasthan. In fact, their deeds have become an integral part of the region's history and public memory. Steadfast in their commitment to independence as a political goal, the Ranas exemplified the spirit of righteous defenders of their own values, faith, and territories without being needlessly aggressive or acquisitive.

• • •

The Custodian and the Crown:

At the time of independence in 1947, India comprised nearly 565 independent Princely States. Mewar was neither the richest nor the largest of the Princely States. In terms of sheer wealth and power, Hyderabad, Mysore, Gwalior, Jamnagar, Kashmir, and others were far greater. Yet Mewar was acknowledged as the "most respected".

During colonial rule, the Maharanas of Mewar knew how to survive difficult times, how to plan for and surmount the financial challenges they often had to face. Being fiercely independent, they did not succumb to the machinations of British Imperial rulers. The historical episode most often narrated is one of Maharana Fateh Singh who "refused" to partake in the Delhi Durbars of 1903 and 1911, which were held to showcase the might of British Imperialism over the Sovereign Princely States of India. In his own quiet and unassuming way, he made the visiting British King realise that Mewar could not be equated with any of the other Princely States. He made his point of independence and honour without creating a conflict or controversy. In 2011, Shriji Arvind Singh Mewar, great-grandson of Maharana Fateh Singh and the seventy-sixth Custodian of the House, recounted the story of how the Maharana stood his ground. "In every way, Maharana Fateh Singh was an honourable Custodian, upholding the flame of freedom just as his forefathers had done. For me, he remains a quintessential upholder of India's dignity, and the spirit of autonomy in our House."

• • •

Mewar and National honour:

Independence from British rule came with the Partition of India: up to 500,000 people died as a consequence of the Partition as fourteen million Hindus, Sikhs and Muslims were displaced from their homes. It was the largest mass migration in history. At that time, the State of Mewar, which was relatively untouched by the traumas of the Partition, became the first Princely State to integrate Mewar with the Union of India. It was a voluntary act reflecting Mewar's deep understanding that a strong and unified India was more important than mere regional independence. Maharana Bhupal Singh, the Custodian of Mewar in 1947, said on that historic occasion, "Today is a day of which I am extremely proud. India is independent. It brings to fulfilment our 1,400 year struggle and the endeavours of my forefathers. It becomes my sacred duty to merge our cherished and sacred Flame of Freedom with that of the free and independent Union of India."

With its accession to the Republic of India, Mewar ceased to exist as a sovereign State. Its economy, polity, administration, judiciary, palaces, public buildings, lands, and resources were merged with or handed over to the State of India. Members of the Royal House of Mewar had become citizens of the democratic Republic of India. The Maharanas, as Custodians of the House of Mewar, continued to work on socially relevant projects involving the community, voluntarily discharging their moral and social duties as Custodians. In the 1950s and 1960s Maharana Bhagwat Singh, the seventy-fifth Custodian of the House, initiated development projects in Udaipur's City Palace to provide employment for the people. He began the process of transitioning the Princely State of Mewar towards a modern self-sustaining House.

• • •

Establishing the Foundation:

In 1969 Maharana Bhagwat Singh announced the formation of the Maharana of Mewar Charitable Foundation. He donated large portions of the City Palace of Udaipu, along with an endowment, to the Foundation. The City Palace became a museum open to the public, and sustained by fees from visitors.

The Maharana's decision proved to be an act of foresight and strategic thinking. In 1971, the twenty-sixth Amendment to the Constitution of India abolished all Princely Privileges. The era of the Princely States ended with a stroke of the pen. Maharana Bhagwat Singh was unfazed by a scenario that could look bleak to others, having built platforms for future growth by creating charitable trusts. Education, community welfare, philanthropy, and heritage preservation remained focus areas. He wanted to ensure not just the continuity and perpetuity of the House of Mewar but its core principle of governance through Custodianship.

His endeavours resulted in revenue generation for public charities from otherwise "immovable and unproductive" assets like palaces and public buildings. The City Palace Museum, the Maharana Mewar Public School, and the Shri Vidyadan Trust are some of the enduring institutions that continue to flourish. In the twenty-first century, these institutions directly employ over 2,000 people, indirectly generating employment for 5,000 families of the heritage-city Udaipur.

• • •

Modern times, modern solutions:

Maharana Bhagwat Singh wrote another glorious chapter in the continuing transition of the House of Mewar in the twentieth century. In early 1960, he converted Jag Niwas Palace into the Lake Palace Hotel. Having travelled widely in Europe and the United States, he was able to gauge the potential of heritage tourism in India. Through his visionary decision to convert the island-palace, he showed almost every former Royal House in India the blueprint for preserving heritage and generating revenues through tourism. "With this one key decision, he put Udaipur on the international tourism map where it has remained to date," commented Shriji.

Since the pioneering years of Maharana Bhagwat Singh, the HRH Group of Hotels in Udaipur has covered much ground. It is the flagship commercial venture of the House of Mewar, and India's only chain of heritage palace-hotels and resorts under private ownership. As Chairman and Managing Director of the HRH Group, Shriji Arvind Singh Mewar said, "In our palace-hotels and retreats, through our museums and collections, we are continuing the traditions of Mewar's Royal past, yet making them contemporary and relevant for a global audience. I call it the challenge of 'Living Heritage'."

Since 2012, the HRH Group of Hotels and the Maharana of Mewar Charitable Foundation, in association with UNESCO India, have jointly organised the World Living Heritage Festival, the first of its kind in India. This festival facilitates the development of Udaipur beyond just a "tourist destination": as a heritage-city, Udaipur reaffirms its identity as a centre for excellence in heritage management, hospitality, education, performing arts, fine arts, environmentalism, and sports. The festival also provides an answer to the question: "Can these unchanging values help Mewar build a bridge between a historic past and a VUCA (volatile, uncertain, complex and ambiguous) future?" The answer is a resounding 'Yes'!"

Bortolo Nardini, Distilleria a Vapore
ITALY

Still managed by descendants of the original family, this distillery is the world's oldest grappa producer.

1779

Nardini acquavit (grappa) has been produced and bottled in Bassano del Grappa, in the northeastern part of Italy since 1779. The founder of the distillery, Bortolo Nardini, bought an inn at the entrance of the wooden, covered Palladian Bassano bridge. The inn became the Grapperia Nardini, strategically located for both the ample water supply, a necessary element in the distillation process, as well as its accessibility to the local regional markets.

The grappa produced by Nardini not only appealed to the taste of the people of Bassano but also to that of the business travellers passing through the area. In only a few years, it became a tradition to have a *cicheto* (local measure in a shot glass) of grappa before continuing the voyage, or to celebrate the closing of a business deal.

As the Grapperia Nardini is preserved in its original state, it is included in the exclusive Association of Historical Places of Italy.

In 2004, the Nardini family celebrated its 225th year by unveiling the Bolle visitor centre, welcoming all who are interested in grappa and its culture.

Today

Nardini has two distilleries, and a bottling facility. It has a 25 per cent share of the global market, and produces four million bottles a year. Still run by Bortolo Nardini's descendants, the firm is the world's oldest grappa producer.

The goals that Nardini has achieved over time, such as innovative distillation techniques, are fruits of its heritage based on values intrinsic to the history of the Nardini family. Values inspired by a strong work ethic, the constant search for excellence and social responsibility, tenets that are cherished to this day.

ANTONIO GUARDA NARDINI
Chief Executive Officer

After the fall of the Venetian republic, and alternating French and Austrian occupation, the city of Bassano became one of the backdrops of the two world wars. Despite the destruction caused by the wars, the grapperia kept working without interruption. In these years, the Nardini Company overcame the difficulties caused by the war, and countless troops marching through, and alcoholic drinks being frequently confiscated by the army. The Second World War saw the Germans destroying Bassano's strategic Old Bridge but luckily Nardini's grapperia and attached production centre escaped major damage. After the war, Italian Alpini soldiers painstakingly reconstructed the wooden pontoon bridge according to Andrea Palladio's original 1569 design.

• • •

Grappa Nardini is produced in two distilleries: one in Bassano del Grappa, and one in Monastier, both in the Veneto Region, in northern Italy. Grappa, obtained from the distillation of grape pomace, is the traditional and only Italian spirit. The destalked grape pomace is stored in the distillery within twenty-four hours after pressing for wine production, following a process of natural fermentation, in an airtight condition, and without the aid of yeast that would lessen the quality of the final distillate. Distillation takes place in autumn, following the harvest season. In Bassano, distillation takes place in a traditional pot still. The water vapour is forced through the naturally fermented grape pomace, in a vacuum-sealed system, which allows a lower distillation temperature, and avoids overheating of the pomace that would irreparably damage the taste and aroma profile of the final product. In Monastier, the continuous steam distilling technique is used, resulting in a clean and balanced taste of the final spirit. The product obtained from the two distilleries is then manually blended to guarantee a consistent tasting and aromatic profile.

• • •

Nardini has introduced many innovations, one of which is the ageing of its grappa. Popular not only in Italy but also abroad, the British Queen Mother served aged Nardini grappa in 1953 at the reception for the coronation of her daughter Elizabeth II — a prestigious acknowledgement of Italian excellence!

• • •

As an environmentally-conscious company, Nardini has adopted a system for re-use of the distilled pomace, and its transformation into new resources. After distillation, the pomace is recovered and dried to separate its components, which are later utilised in the cosmetic, food, and animal feed industries.

• • •

Nardini's grappa label has remained almost unchanged since it was designed in 1779, and is an early example of subliminal marketing: The word Bassano set boldly, and with a slight space between the double "s" and an "x" above, so as to draw the eye to the word "sano" — underlining its therapeutic and curative properties. In addition, Bortolo Nardini labelled his grappa Aquavite di Vinacchia, spelling acquavite the Latin style, without the letter "c", and using the play on the word acquavite meaning both distillate and water of life. This name is still featured on the Italian labels produced today.

• • •

The Nardini family believes the ritual of drinking is deeply connected with balance and quality. Together with seven of Italy's most prominent family-run distilleries and liqueur makers, they established the Spirit of Italy, a project for publicizing Italian quality abroad. The Spirit of Italy stands for culture, lifestyle, and research, and was conceived in collaboration with great mixologists, to bring the culture of taste and new interpretation of tradition to the export market.

• • •

A 225th anniversary is worth marking in style, so the Nardini family commissioned the architect Massimiliano Fuksas to design what he calls Bolle (bubbles). Fuksas first presented the space-age design, shaped to look like two drops coming off a still, drawn on a dining plate at a restaurant in Bassano. The contemporary building took two years to plan, and another two years to build. It incorporates a research laboratory, auditorium and visitor centre, and is built from materials used in grappa production: glass (bottles), steel (storage silos), water, and wood (for the ageing process).
The Nardini family has always been linked with culture, and therefore, numerous events are held at Bolle. In addition, the family has established global cultural partnerships, and the Nardini Garage, in the town of Bassano del Grappa, which brings together the local community by hosting artists, and showcasing Italian and international creativity.

Antica Corte Pallavicina, Culatello di Zibello DOP

ITALY

The oldest producer of Culatello, the firm has secured a DOP for this cured meat delicacy and forced the industry to apply production techniques that date back centuries.

1735

In the cellars of the old fortified castle built by the Pallavicini family in 1320, the Marquises had for centuries practised the art of Culatello di Zibello production. Although there are many unofficial accounts of when the Culatello production started, an unambiguous mention of the Culatello is to be found in a 1735 document of Parma Municipium, the *Calmiero della Carne Porcina Salata*.

With just 30,000 hams produced a year, compared with almost ten million *prosciutti di Parma*, the Culatello is sold only to the very best shops and restaurants worldwide. In the Bassa Parmense, a lowland farming area along the muddy River Po northwest of Parma, only a handful of artisans are allowed to make the hams labelled Culatello di Zibello DOP (Protected Designation of Origin).

Today

Today, the fourth generation of the Spigaroli family is responsible for the Culatello production at Antica Corte Pallavicina. The owner, Massimo Spigaroli, is the high priest of the Culatello artisans.

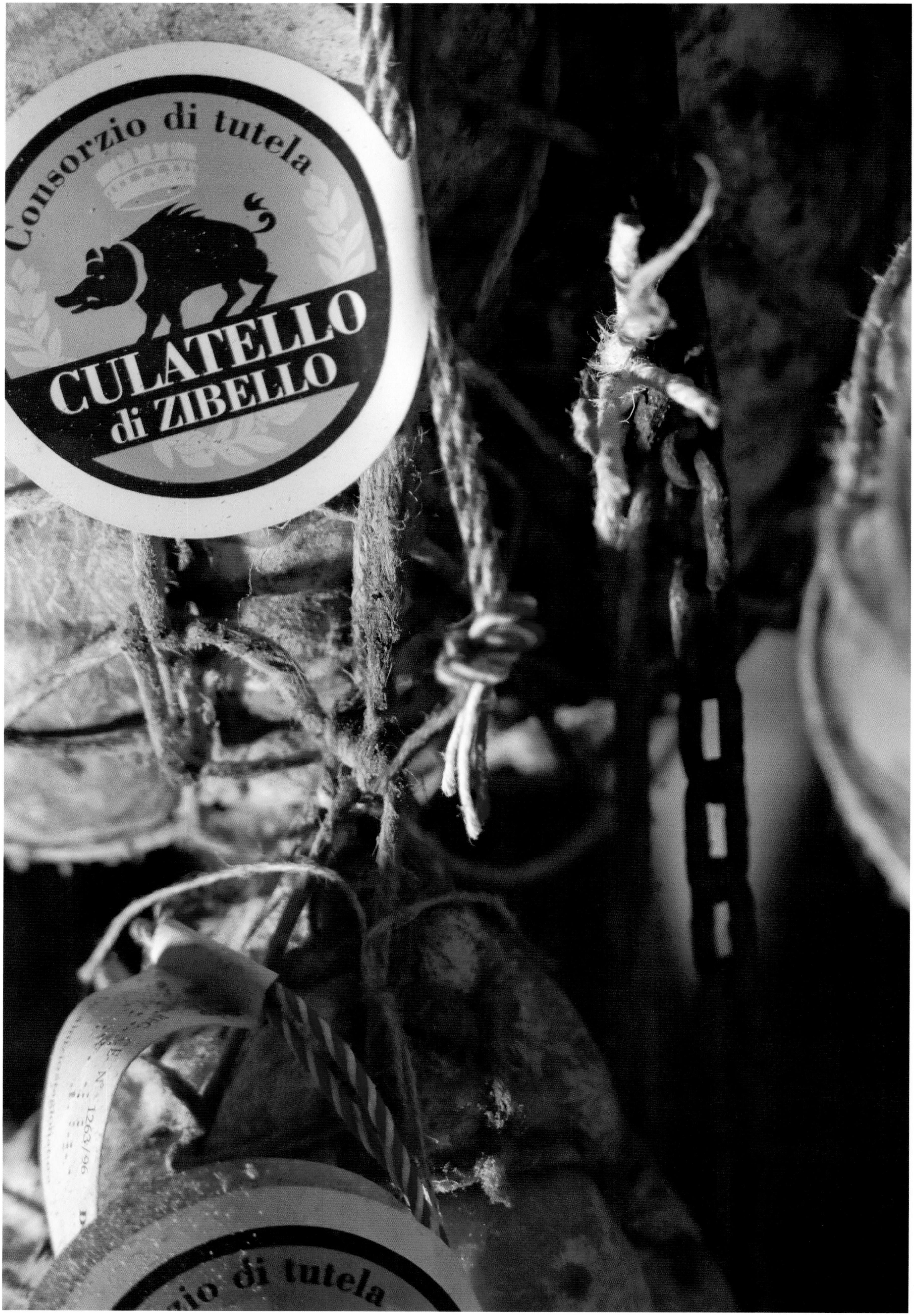
Consorzio di tutela
CULATELLO
di ZIBELLO
di tutela

When EU health inspectors started complaining about the traditional practice of exposing raw meat to river mists, Culatello was about to join the dodo. We sprang into action and secured a DOP (Protected Designation of Origin) for Culatello. The Spigaroli family headed the Culatello di Zibello Consortium to enforce the use of production techniques that dated back centuries. Today, thanks in large part to our family, Culatello's fame is spreading beyond Italy – with mixed results. Some producers are beginning to forsake the consortium rules for more relaxed DOP guidelines, and food giants from surrounding regions have entered the game, curing their hams in high-tech facilities for fourteen months at most. How long before Culatello ends up bastardised, like aceto balsamico?

MASSIMO SPIGAROLI
Owner

That Parma has a native talent for processing pork is shown not only by prosciutto, which is typical of hilly areas where the dry climate plays an essential part in drying it, but also by Culatello, a cured meat of the humid lowlands. Culatello means "little ass", and is obtained from the top part of the sectioned leg.

• • •

The Antica Corte Pallavicina's customers include not only some of the world's greatest chefs but also the Prince of Wales. The royal porcophile was introduced to Spigaroli's handiwork by his advisors on pig farming, who told him that his Large Black and Tamworth pigs were good only for bacon and sausages. Could Spigaroli, they wondered, help the prince to improve quality, and cure salami on the spot for him, in Britain? But the answer was an unequivocal no. The royal porkers' meat must be sent to Bassa Parmense for curing. The hams need their mould, their old curing cellars, and their Po fog.

• • •

Culatello production begins during the winter months; local pigs that have been fattened on legumes and grains are used. Once the hind leg is boned and divided, the Culatello is massaged for several days, first with garlic and wine, then with salt and pepper. Packed in a clean pig's bladder and bundled tightly with twine, the meat does a stint in a cool, dry cantina before cellaring for fourteen to forty-eight months.
The Culatello needs constant minding: the *salumaio* must know exactly when to open and close the cellar windows to the misty Po breezes in order to aid the formation of *muffa nobile*, or noble mould, and keep away excessive heat and humidity. The hams must also be rotated around the cellar every few months.
As the ham ages, it loses up to half its moisture and weight while gaining in flavour. At twenty months, the meat is delicate and perfumed; at twenty-seven months, moisture loss gives it a stronger, saltier character; at thirty-six months, the brine has mellowed into a sweetish multidimensional savour.

• • •

A pig is like a Verdi score: you can't get rid of anything. As it happens, the great composer lived just down the road, and got a couple of Culatello as a special Christmas offering from the Antica Corte Pallavicina. Culatello was always precious and the *contadino* never got to taste it himself. Instead, producers would barter one ham for a whole pig or give it as a gift to local worthies. It was the Rolex, the Cartier, of edibles.

{Antica Corte Pallavicina, Culatello di Zibello DOP}

PAULY & C. / CVM
Fondamenta Vetrai Murano
ITALY

The oldest imprint in Murano glassmaking history, the company has an unrivalled reputation for innovation and a clientele of royalty and celebrities.

For centuries

Run as a family business for hundreds of years, Pauly & C. / CVM today is the oldest imprint for glass in Murano's history. From the thirteenth to the eighteenth century, Murano was one of the wonders of the world with an unrivalled reputation for innovation, its glassmakers having developed, among other things, ways of incorporating threads of gold into their creations, and techniques for the famous millefiori (multi-coloured) and lattimo (milk) glass.

1919

The company name derives from the merger in 1919 of Pauly & C. and the Compagnia di Venezia e Murano. The company also incorporates the prestigious brand MVM Cappellin & C., which was acquired in 1932, and owns the drawings and back catalogues of the renowned glass blowers Toso Vetri d'Arte, acquired in 1990.

We take pride in all our products being one hundred per cent "Made in Italy": all our staff is from Italy, and the artwork is produced exclusively in Venice / Murano. One of our challenges today is the recruitment of qualified artisans. Another challenge is to compete with mass-produced products. In response, we decided to focus on bespoke pieces. Even drinking glasses, today a commoditised product, can, in some instances, become a customised work of art – some were recently ordered by the President of Azerbaijan.

DR MAX BOSCARO
Chief Executive Officer

Success was crowned in 1872 when, after almost two thousand years, Vincenzo Moretti, alongside the brothers Alessandro and Augusto Castellani, revived the ancient technique, reproducing the type of Roman glass that would come to be known all over the world as the "murrine". In 1878, the Compagnia di Venezia e Murano presented the "murrine" at the International Exhibition in Paris. Its success was such that the "murrine" became the company's most sought-after article, and it would become the symbol of glass production in Venice.

• • •

When the Murano glass economy was in crisis, and when many of the traditional production techniques had been lost, Pauly & C. / CVM invested substantial sums of money in reviving them, and in training master glassblowers, establishing for them a school of design at which attendance was compulsory. Painters and engravers were brought in from Rome, London and Paris to apply their craft to glass production techniques.

• • •

Remaining true to its historic roots, at a time when Murano glass production has become increasingly industrialised and many glassworks have begun churning out cheap mass-produced products, Pauly & C. / CVM has continued to concentrate on a uniquely artisan production, and has strengthened its ties with the best master glassblowers in Murano, and with international artists in order to satisfy an increasingly demanding clientele looking for a piece of history, quality and luxury.

• • •

During its long history, Pauly & C. /CVM has served an international client base that includes some prominent names such as the writer Arthur Conan Doyle, the fashion designer Miuccia Prada; the actors Antony Hopkins and Jack Nicholson, the actress Catherine Deneuve, the singer Elton John, the director Federico Fellini and his wife Giulietta Masina; figures from the world of industry and finance such as the Agnelli family, the Rockefeller family, the Pirelli family; politicians and nobility: the American presidents Theodore and Franklin Delano Roosevelt, the Berlusconi family and the Russian Imperial family. In addition, the list includes museums such as the New York Metropolitan Museum of Art and the Victoria & Albert Museum.

• • •

Of particular historical significance is the monumental Venetian crystal centrepiece in the shape of an Italian-style garden, produced in 1931, and still owned by Pauly & C. /CVM, which was used by the Fascist regime, and Benito Mussolini during Hitler's trip to Italy, when it was placed in the conference room where the two men met.

• • •

In developing products, Pauly & C. /CVM has availed itself of the genius of artists such as Alfredo Barbini, Lucio Bubacco, Romeo Gigli, Berit Johansson, Livio de Marchi, Napoleone Martinuzzi, Aristide Najean, Franz Pratti, Mariagrazia Rosin, Xiao Fan Ru, Enzo Scarpa, Oliviero Toscani, and Libero Vitali.

• • •

Pauly C. / CVM has been creating pieces for the principal European palaces since the 1950s. These have included the six-metre high chandelier created for the Palazzo del Quirinale in Rome, the official home of the President of the Italian Republic; the chandelier for the Vatican Palace, also in Rome, the chandelier for the Royal Palace in Copenhagen and one for the Hotel Royal Danieli in Venice. For the lighting system of the residential neighbourhood of Kuwait City, and the Al Assawi family palace, a magnificent "Rezzonico" chandelier, six metres high, four metres wide, and with 320 lights, was designed and installed in the main salon.

Rahn & Bodmer Co., Private Bank

SWITZERLAND

The oldest bank in Switzerland belongs to an exclusive circle of non-listed, owner-managed Swiss Private Banks.

In the banking world, there will always be conglomerates, which are successful in achieving economies of scale, and standardising products and services. There will also always be space for independent private banks, which put their trust in individuality, client proximity and continuity. As private bankers, we are entrepreneurs, who secure the financial stability of the Zurich Private Bank Rahn & Bodmer Co. with our personal assets. It follows that we five partners are all as equally interested in the smooth running of the business as our clients. Aiming to build on the trust of our clients over generations, we place great value on continuity in client support, business policies as well as the management of our family business. In doing so, we can stay faithful to values, which have been sustained over generations.

MARTIN H. BIDERMANN

Partner

In contrast to great financial centres such as Amsterdam or London, it took a relatively long time for commercial banks to become established in Switzerland. In 1850 there was still not a single major bank in Switzerland. It was not until the railways were built that there was a great upturn for corporate lending businesses, stock trading, and the issuing of shares. Nor were other types of banks founded until the nineteenth century. The so-called spring of savings banks did not begin until the end of the Napoleonic War in 1815. The first cantonal banks arose in the aftermath of the liberal revolutions in certain cantons in the 1830s, and in the decade of the Democratic Movement in the 1860s.

The Private Bank Rahn & Bodmer Co. may call itself the oldest bank in Switzerland, since it was customary in the eighteenth century for trade and banking business to be combined.

• • •

The founding and development of the Private Bank Rahn & Bodmer Co. took place during a particularly turbulent time. Neither the effects of the Seven Years' War, nor of the French Revolution, early industrialisation, the global economic crisis, the First or Second World Wars or the oil crisis left it unscathed. By the turn of the millennium, there were only a few sectors that had faced as many challenges within a short space of time as had banking. As a result of the financial crisis and the tax debate, the banking system has had to face a regulatory torrent that has left it little room for manoeuvre, and piled up more and more rules for it to comply with.

• • •

Clean money strategies and the automatic exchange of information present clients with the question as to how confidential the handling of their personal data still is, and foreign nationals face almost unlimited scrutiny. Bank-client confidentiality came into effect in Switzerland in 1935, but it is not peculiar to Switzerland alone; other countries maintain confidentiality between banks and their clients. Critics claim that the dilution of bank-client confidentiality has made Switzerland less attractive as a banking centre, and that new centres are overtaking Zurich and Geneva. Nevertheless, no other country has managed to acquire a position in global asset management as strong as Switzerland.

• • •

Despite great changes, Switzerland is still the global financial centre for the management of private wealth. So there must be other reasons for its rise to prominence and success:

- Strong economy: Switzerland is still one of the most competitive countries in the world, and, in terms of its population, has the most international large companies, as well as many small and medium-sized enterprises, which are global leaders in their fields.
- Healthy state finances: Hardly any European country has a state debt as low and a budget as balanced as Switzerland's.
- Prosperity: The strong economy and healthy state budget have made a one-time poor alpine republic a prosperous country with worldwide peak values in income and assets.
- Political stability: Direct democracy and the consensus system means that decisions are generally balanced out, and present few surprises.
- First-class infrastructure: In terms of traffic links, energy provision, communications and building quality, Switzerland has one of the most solid infrastructures in the world.

There are other factors that have made Switzerland successful as a financial centre: A strong education system, successful research and development in worldwide leading universities, a modern health service, and its position in central Europe.

Teatro alla Scala

ITALY

The institution is one of the principal opera houses in the world and has provided the stage for historic productions as well as some scandals.

1778

La Scala, or the "Teatro alla Scala" theatre in Milan, is one of the principal opera houses of the world.

Built from 1776-1778 by the Empress Maria Theresa of Austria (whose country then ruled Milan), it replaced an earlier theatre that had burned down. In 1872 it became the property of the city of Milan. The house was closed during the First World War. In 1920, the conductor Arturo Toscanini led a council that raised money to reopen it, organising it as an autonomous corporation. Bombed during the Second World War, the theatre reopened in 1946, partly through funds raised by benefit concerts given by Toscanini. In late 2001 La Scala closed for extensive renovations. Mario Botta served as the architect on the project, and the theatre reopened in December 2004 with a performance of Antonio Salieri's *Europa Riconosciuta*, which had been performed at La Scala's opening on 3 August 1778.

Today

La Scala is home to the La Scala Theatre Chorus, La Scala Theatre Ballet, and La Scala Theatre Orchestra. The theatre also has an associated school known as the La Scala Theatre Academy, which offers professional training in music, dance, stagecraft, and stage management.

VIETATO L'ACCESS
ALLE VIE DI CORS

TEATRO ALLA SCALA

Fondazione di diritto privato

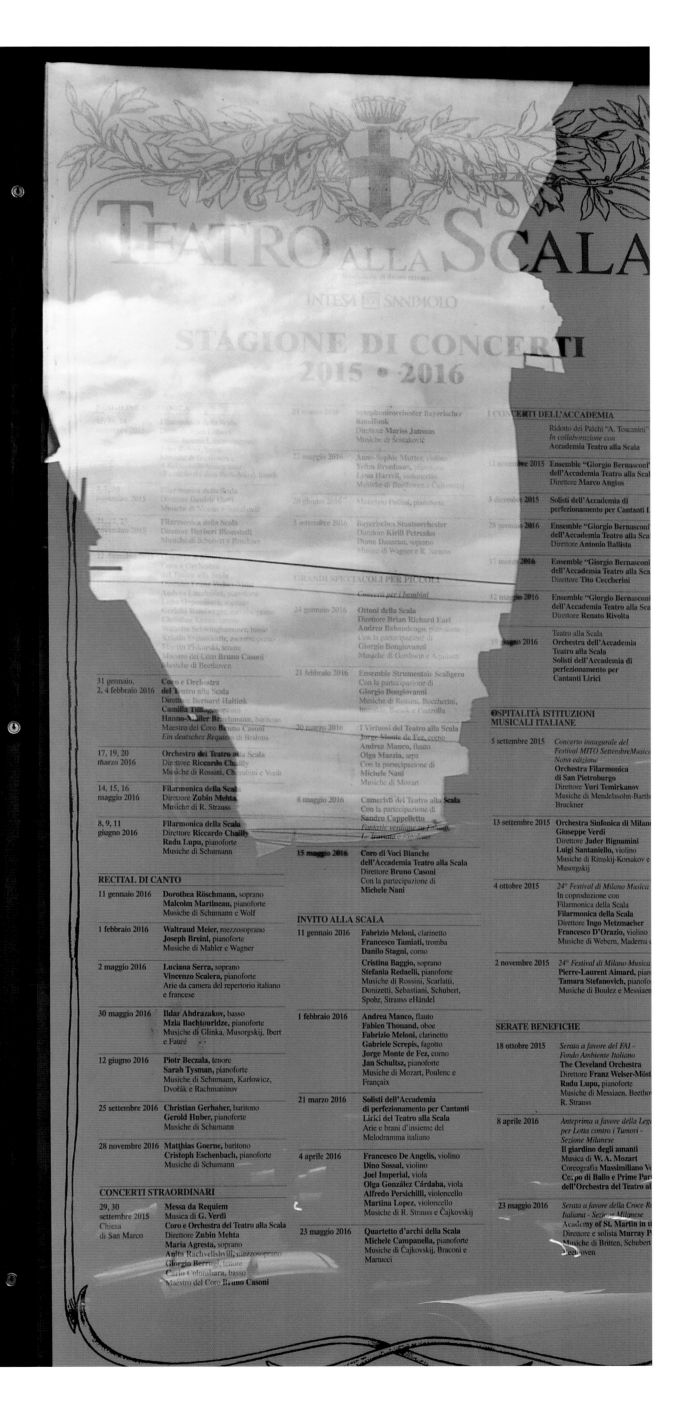

A fire destroyed the previous theatre, the Teatro Regio Ducale, on 25 February 1776, after a carnival gala. A group of ninety wealthy Milanese, who owned *palchi* (private boxes) in the theatre, wrote to Archduke Ferdinand of Austria-Este asking for a new theatre, and a provisional one to be used while completing the new one. The initial design was rejected but the second plan was accepted by Empress Maria Theresa. The new theatre was built on the former location of the church of Santa Maria alla Scala, from which the theatre gets its name. The church was deconsecrated and demolished, and the theatre was completed over a period of two years.

• • •

Soon after its inauguration, La Scala became the preeminent meeting place for noble and wealthy Milanese families. In the tradition of the times, the *platea* (the main floor) had no chairs and spectators watched the shows standing up. The orchestra was in full sight, as the *golfo mistico* (orchestra pit) had not yet been built. Above the boxes, La Scala has a gallery where the less wealthy could watch the performances. The gallery is typically crowded with the most critical opera aficionados, known as the *loggionisti*, who can be ecstatic or merciless towards singers' perceived successes or failures. For their failures, artists receive a "baptism of fire" from these aficionados, and fiascos are long remembered. As an example, in 2006, the tenor Roberto Alagna was booed off the stage during a performance of *Aida,* with the result that his understudy, Antonello Palombi, quickly replaced him mid-scene without time to change into a costume.

• • •

As with most theatres in the nineteenth century, La Scala was also a casino, with gamblers sitting in the foyer. Conditions in the auditorium, could also be frustrating for the opera lover, as described in 1840: "At the Opera they were performing Otto Nicolai's *Templario*. Unfortunately… the theatre served not only as the universal drawing-room for all Milan's society, but every sort of trading transaction, from horse dealing to stock-jobbing, was carried on in the pit, so that one could catch only bits of the melody."

• • •

La Scala hosted the *prima* (first production) of many famous operas, and had a special relationship with Verdi. For several years, however, he did not allow his work to be performed at La Scala, as some of his music had been modified (he said "corrupted") by the orchestra. This dispute originated in a disagreement over the production of his *Giovanna d'Arco* in 1845. However, Verdi later conducted his *Requiem* there on 25 May 1874, and in 1886 announced that La Scala would host the premiere of what was to become his penultimate opera, *Otello*. The premiere of his last opera, *Falstaff*, was also given in the theatre.

• • •

The renovation by renowned architect Mario Botta proved controversial, as preservationists feared that historic details would be lost. However, the opera company was said to be impressed with the improvements to the structure and the sound quality, which was enhanced by the removal of the heavy red carpets in the hall. The stage was entirely reconstructed, and an enlarged backstage area allowed more sets to be stored, facilitating more productions.

• • •

La Scala has instituted a new programme for children's opera, introduced low-cost tickets to draw an untapped audience of opera lovers, initiated a Puccini cycle, and developed programming to explore composers of Italian verismo, the "realistic" style of opera that emerged in the late nineteenth century, and added non-Italian composers to the programme, who have not been well represented up till now. Children's opera proved a success. At first, 20,000 tickets were offered to the community for shortened versions of children-friendly operas like *Cinderella*, and they sold out immediately.

The credo of La Scala is to concentrate on a very important part of its opera patrimony. That is why half the operas should be Italian operas. This is not a provincial perspective. La Scala must show its heritage in Italian opera, including that of the early nineteenth and twentieth centuries.

Zunft zur Schmiden
SWITZERLAND

Members of this ancient Swiss guild still practice the
traditional smithy's craft.

1336

Summary of different groups of jobs in the Zunft zur Schmiden (Smiths' Guild): smiths, swordsmiths (weapons), pewterers (plates/dishes), metalworkers (cow and church bells), tinsmiths and armourers (chainmail shirts). A century later, in 1433, the Scherer society (basic surgery, treating dislocated limbs) and the Bader society (massage, cupping, stitching wounds) were integrated into the Zunft zur Schmiden. About a hundred years later, the Scherers and Baders found their own premises for practising their skills.

1412

Purchase of the guild house "Zum goldenen Horn", the oldest guild house in the world, which has always remained the property of the Zunft zur Schmiden in spite of the French Revolution and economic crises.

1798

French (Helvetic) Revolution: members of the Zunft zur Schmiden shared the guild's assets amongst themselves rather than handing them over to the "liberators of our country". In the following year, the French regiment's tailors were lodged in the guild house.

1975

The "Handwerk der Schmide" ("Smiths' Craft") association was founded and blacksmiths' work was actively resumed.

It's important to us that the craft guild should continue to develop, not only through the recruitment of new guildsmen but also, among other things, by maintaining contact and friendly relations with other guilds. The Zunft zur Schmiden is constituted of 150 guild certificates – in essence one share certificate per guild member. Succession is in two stages: in the first, sons, sons-in-law and grandsons can be accepted; in the second, friends of guild members may be invited to join.

THOMAS R. LIMBURG
Guild Guardian

The first Alemannic guilds emerged in the fourteenth century. Beyond the commercial components, the guilds formed an all-embracing community founded on custom and tradition, including not only masters, but also journeymen, apprentices, women and children. A widow stayed in the guild with her business operation until she remarried or could be succeeded by a son. The guild was also an army unit and served as a basis for organising guard duty and wartime military service.

• • •

Some outstanding figures from Zurich's history have been involved with the Zunft zur Schmiden (Smiths' Guild) over the centuries and to this day. One example is Johann Heinrich Pestalozzi (1746–1827), known for his work with needy children and their education. His ideas about reforming the education of young people found no favour in the old Confederation. Pestalozzi was a supporter of the French Revolution and was the only Swiss honorary citizen of the French Republic. Teaching methods were his first priority, but with the growth of industrialisation, thoughts of social reform were seen as destructive to the family unit.

• • •

After the guilds' privileges were abolished following a referendum in 1838, the Zunft zur Schmiden held a symbolic "guild funeral" on the Lindenhof in Zurich. Banners and glasses were buried along with a bottle of wine. The following year, in memory of the burial of the Zunft zur Schmiden, all the guilds joined in marking the anniversary with the first-ever festive Sechseläuten procession. The annual Sechseläuten procession has become a unique historical celebration. There's an authenticity about it because it's typical of old traditions: most guilds wear their historical costumes for the procession.

• • •

On the occasion of a smiths' course in 1975, the idea of setting up a smithy owned by the guild itself came up, the object being to resurrect and regularly practise the Zunft zur Schmiden's ancient craft. The four forges, many oil and electric-powered ovens, mechanical hammers and other furnishings from a bygone age make the place seem, at first sight, like a museum. But as soon as the fires get going, it becomes clear that there's real forging work going on here.

Schwabe Verlag AG

SWITZERLAND

Established more than 500 years ago, this printing house was the first to publish the New Testament in German.

1488

The printing business was founded by Johannes Petri (born 1441) of Langendorf near Hammelburg, Franconia, who had learned the art of printing and typecasting in Mainz during Gutenberg's lifetime. He settled in Basel, one of the earliest printing centres in the world, after the founding of the University of Basel (1460). The second-generation owner of the printing office was Petri's nephew Adam Petri, who was an eager follower of Martin Luther. He printed almost all of Luther's important works. For example, he was the first in Basel to print the New Testament (1523) as translated by the reformer of Wartburg.

The firm flourished under Adam's son Heinrich Petri (1508–1579), who, in addition to his publishing work, was a councillor of Basel, and deputy to the Confederation. Heinrich Petri steered clear of religious controversy and published literature on theology by classic authors, contemporary history, and books on mathematics and science, medicine and alchemy, among them many compilations and extensive lexicons.

After Heinrich Petri's death, Sebastian Henrich Petri took over the business. In 1665 his heir, Jacob Bertsche, assumed control of the firm, which then passed to the Lüdin family, and later to the Decker family, a printing dynasty, which merged it with the Schweigerhauserische Verlagsbuchhandlung publishing house. After several transformations, the business was taken over by Benno Schwabe in 1868.

Today

Schwabe's descendants ran the company until the end of the twentieth century. In 1996 the majority of the company's shares were owned by Ruedi Bienz and Dr Urs Breitenstein – both long-term directors. After retiring, Dr Urs Breitenstein sold his shares to his equal partner Ruedi Bienz, who is now the sole owner of the Schwabe Company.

I like it ⌀TO 👍

GOTT GRÜSS' DIE KUNST
110
JAHRE
HEIDELBERGER
DRUCKMASCHINEN
1850-1960

ORIGINAL
HEIDELBERG
CYLINDER

56 × 77 cm   22" × 30¼"

In 1500 only the wealthy could afford books. A book cost between two and five guilders, and a bound and illustrated copy was almost twice as expensive as an unbound one. A house in a prime location in Basel cost sixty guilders; the yearly income for a writer was ten guilders.

• • •

Producing the edition of the works of St Augustine was a daring endeavour, not least from a material point of view. The product consisted of eleven volumes made up of 1,275 sheets of paper. One sheet of paper weighed about seven grams, with the final product weighing almost nine kilos (without the book cover). The print run amounted to 2,200 copies; 565 bales of paper were needed, making about twenty tons of paper. At that time, a paper mill could produce an average of 120 to 160 bales of paper a year.

• • •

"Educated unmarried woman of mature age, experienced in massage, nursing and healthcare, linguistically competent, seeks post as assistant at doctor's practice, sanatorium or private clinic. Offer under code B D 5491." Sending her ad to the Schwabe Verlag's Correspondenz-Blatt für Schweizer Aerzte (Correspondence Page for Swiss Doctors) was, for this lady, the right thing to do, since the publication of advertisements was one of the things the specialist magazine set out to do when it was founded in 1870.

• • •

German troops crossed the Polish border on 1 September 1939, just a day after the Swiss Federal Council had announced a general mobilisation. Barricades were set up in Basel, and the borders to Germany were closed. The resources and options available to the Swiss press were becoming more and more limited; a physical presence in Germany was also becoming less and less possible. But at the same time, authors and editors were coming to Switzerland with projects that could no longer be realised in Nazi Germany.

• • •

It was thanks to Walter Muschg, who wanted to offer young talents a platform in the Schweizerische Reihe, that Max Frisch came to Schwabe with the manuscript of the first of his plays to be performed. "I would like to inform you of my immediate approval. Just one small thing, regarding the writing: Swiss poets, written as Schweizerdichter, reminds me of Schweizerware ('Swiss products'), Schweizerkäse ('Swiss cheese'), Schweizerwoche ('Swiss week'), and I'd very much prefer if Professor Muschg as the responsible editor would agree for Schweizer Dichter to be written instead."

• • •

As a careful and responsible patron, the owner thought about his succession well in advance. And so it happened that he invited three young employees to lunch on a November day in 1987. There was no agenda; it was an informal lunch. The guests were excited and a little nervous. And then came a single question from the boss: Did they fancy taking over the business? The incredible offer amounted to a management buy-out. The trio paused before answering enthusiastically: Yes! However, there was a big "but": Where would they get the money from? The boss tersely replied that he had asked about willingness, and not money. A year later the time had come. The three designated successors each received a gift of 8 per cent of the Schwabe shares, laying the foundation for the future.

The oldest major auction house in the world, the firm holds a
number of world records for auctioned works of art, including
Edvard Munch's painting The Scream.

1744

Sotheby's was established on 11 March 1744 in London. Originally British, Sotheby's is today a multinational corporation, headquartered in New York City. One of the world's largest auction houses of fine and decorative art, jewellery, real estate, and collectibles, Sotheby's operations are divided into three segments: auction, finance, and dealer. The company's services range from corporate art services to private sales. Sotheby's has over 1500 employees in ninety locations spread over forty countries, and conducts 250 auctions each year in over seventy categories.

Sotheby's is the world's fourth oldest auction house in continuous operation. Only three auction houses are even older, all in Sweden: Stockholm's Auktionsverk, Gothenburg's Auktionsverk, and Uppsala's Auktionskammare.

The founder, Samuel Baker, was a London bookseller who held his first auction early in 1744, selling 457 valuable books from the library of the Rt Hon Sir John Stanley for a few hundred pounds. He auctioned additional libraries over the years: the library Napoleon took with him into exile on St. Helena, and the library collections of John Wilkes, Benjamin Heywood Bright, and the Dukes of Devonshire and Buckingham were sold through Samuel Baker's auction house. In 1767 Baker went into partnership with George Leigh. Upon Baker's death in 1778, his estate was divided between Leigh and a nephew, John Sotheby, whose successors were to lead the company for more than eighty years until 1861, when the last Sotheby died. The company continued to prosper under a series of partners, and in 1917 moved to the present London quarters at 34-35 New Bond Street.

Throughout the nineteenth and early twentieth centuries, Sotheby's concentrated chiefly on auctioning books, manuscripts, and prints. Although other collectibles were occasionally offered for sale, paintings and other works of art did not begin to dominate Sotheby's sales until after the First World War. Following the Second World War, principally under the leadership of its chairman, from 1958 to 1980, Peter C. Wilson, Sotheby's became established in New York City and, in 1964, acquired Parke-Bernet Galleries, the premier American auction house, founded in 1883. In 1983, a group of investors including American shopping mall developer Alfred Taubman, purchased Sotheby's. Taubman took Sotheby's public in 1988, listing the company's shares on the New York Stock Exchange, which made Sotheby's the oldest publicly traded company on the NYSE.

• • •

The world's most famous paintings, especially old masterworks done before 1803, are generally owned or held at museums. The museums very rarely sell them, and as such, they are quite literally priceless. *Guinness World Records* lists the *Mona Lisa* as having the highest insurance value for a painting in history. On permanent display at *The Louvre* museum in Paris, the *Mona Lisa* was assessed at $100 million on 14 December 1962. Taking inflation into account, the 1962 value would be around $782 million in 2016. Vincent van Gogh, Pablo Picasso, and Andy Warhol have been by far the best represented artists in late twentieth and early twenty-first century auctions of the "most expensive paintings". Whereas Picasso and Warhol became wealthy men, van Gogh (allegedly) sold only one painting in his lifetime, *The Red Vineyard,* for 400 Francs (about $1600) to the impressionist painter and heiress Anna Bloch.

• • •

Sotheby's holds a number of world records for auctioned works of art:

- On 3 May 2006 Sotheby's auctioned Pablo Picasso's *Dora Maar au Chat* for $95 million to an undisclosed purchaser, making it the second most expensive artwork ever sold at an auction at that time.
- Sotheby's holds the world record for the most expensive piece of contemporary art ever sold at an auction, with Mark Rothko's quintessential 1950 *White Center (Yellow, Pink and Lavender on Rose),* which grossed $72.8 million in May 2007.
- On 6 December 2007 Sotheby's auctioned the *Guennol Lioness*, a 3.25-inch limestone lion from ancient Mesopotamia. It is thought to be at least 5,000 years old. It was sold for $75 million, fetching the highest price ever paid at an auction for a sculpture.
- On 15 December 2007 Sotheby's auctioned a limited edition copy of *The Tales of Beedle the Bard* written by J.K. Rowling. Although expected to make just $98,350, the book was purchased for a hammer price of $3,835,980 by London fine art dealers Hazlitt, Gooden and Fox on behalf of Amazon.com.
- On 19 December 2007 Sotheby's auctioned a 710-year-old copy of the *Magna Carta*, the last remaining copy in private hands out of the seventeen that are known to exist. The copy was sold for $21.3 million.
- On 3 February 2010 the sculpture *L'Homme qui marche I* by Alberto Giacometti was sold in London for £65 million ($103.7 million), setting a new world record for a work of art sold at an auction.
- On 2 May 2012 Edvard Munch's painting *The Scream* was sold for $119,922,500, which set another new record.
- On 12 October 2012 the painting *Abstraktes Bild* by Gerhard Richter was sold for $34 million, which set the record for a work by a living artist.

Torrini
ITALY

The oldest goldsmith family, and one of the ten oldest family businesses in the world, has pioneered a finishing technique for gold referred to as oro nativo.

1369

The House of Torrini is the oldest goldsmith family and one of the ten oldest family businesses in the world. The trademark was registered by Jacopus Turini in 1369. In the State Archive of Florence, there is a reference to the Guild of Ironwrights, Armourers and Nailmakers with a seal that is still used today to mark the works that come out of the Manifattura Orafa Torrini.

The historic Torrini shop in the centre of Florence at the Piazza del Duomo was opened in 1919. The venue reflects the heritage of the Torrini dynasty, and offers the public access to myriad examples of the goldsmith's art and skills. The Museum Torrini in Scarperia is an integral part of the Historical Archive Torrini 1369. The museum displays rare examples of Renaissance silverware, which are periodically shown in travelling exhibitions devoted to monographic themes or to particular artists. The collection consists of over 12,000 models that the Manifattura Orafa Torrini has produced over time.

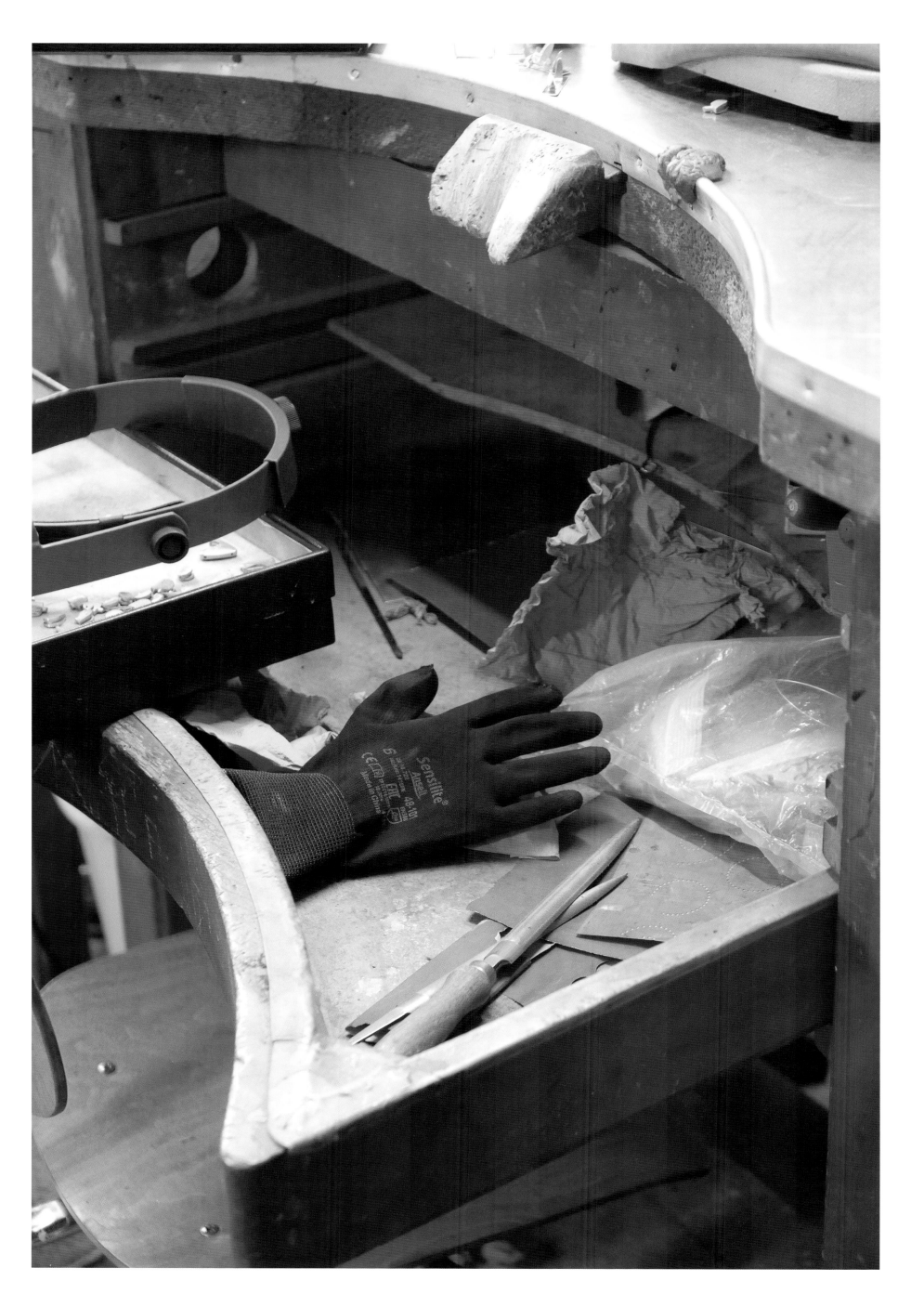

The Torrinis expanded the goldsmith's tradition by combining the world of jewellery with the world of art, and together with well-known artists, created designs to exploit the potential of precious metals and stones. Like a modern Renaissance workshop, Torrini develops designs that are crafted by highly skilled goldsmiths using modern techniques. Refined and exclusive jewellery is the fruit of ancient tradition combined with contemporary creativity: Torrini produces new jewellery which reflects the long heritage of this family of goldsmiths.

FABRIZIO TORRINI
Twenty-fifth Generation

In Italy, the past survives in the present day: the country's allure springs from its enduring history. The renown of Italy's jewellery, with its sensual beauty and extraordinary craftsmanship, is founded on the goldsmithing skills passed down through generations from the medieval guilds that once guarded the secrets of the trade.

The history of the Torrini dynasty started with Jacopus Turini, a skilled craftsman from Scarperia, who moved to Florence in 1369 to register his trademark with the Guild of Ironwrights, Armourers and Nailmakers. Jacopus worked together with his father and brother in the workshop, where they crafted fine suits of armour for the knights of the land. For his seal, Jacopus cleverly combined a spur, symbolising the armour, and half a clover, symbolising the good luck he wished his business to have.

This was the golden age of Italy and Jacopus Turini's business flourished. He decided to specialise in gold and to expand his offering into fine jewellery including bespoke items for his clientele. He also changed the family name to Torrini.

The family fame spread beyond Florence, and members were called to Siena to assist in the construction of its Duomo (cathedral). The Baptismal Font in the Baptistery of Siena has been recognised as a masterpiece, and the bronze reliefs are counted among those of the greatest artists of the time. As a result, the Torrinis were granted the prestigious ecclesiastical title of "Prior" of Siena twenty-eight times, and thus became Siena nobility in the middle of the fifteenth century. When construction of the Siena Duomo was completed around 1500, the Torrinis moved back to their native region of Scarperia to avoid the conflict between the Guelphs and the Ghibellines, and in the eighteenth century, the family returned to Florence.

• • •

Associated with Italian jewellery for over six hundred years, the Torrini dynasty has created a long line of fine jewellery with distinctive textures and vibrant hues, much of which is found in museums for the public to admire.

Perhaps the family's most valued possession is a finishing technique referred to as *oro nativo*, which can be translated as "native gold": this is a method of working with gold so that it retains its natural colour. This technique was derived from the writings of the goldsmith and sculptor Benevenuto Cellini, who used a dipping solution to enhance the natural colour of the metal. The Torrini goldsmiths still use this technique for finishing their jewellery: it has become the quintessential facet of Torrini design.

Hotel Les Trois Rois
SWITZERLAND

Founded as a gentlemen's club, the luxury hotel is one of the oldest in Europe.

1681

The gentlemen's club Drei Könige (Three Kings) in Basel is documented for the first time. It is close to arterial roads for public and trade transport across water and land. Drei Könige is a popular name for pubs and taverns near trade routes. It alludes to the three Wise Men from the East in the Christmas story, commonly known as Kaspar, Melchior and Balthasar.

1797-98

In 1797 General Napoleon Bonaparte stopped at the Drei Könige while travelling, and was honoured with a splendid official reception. The following year, though, under French occupation, kings were not wanted. The guesthouse was renamed Zu den drei Bildern, or Hotel aux trois magots.

1841-42

Over the course of the century, the owners of the guesthouse combined different buildings, mostly former aristocratic residences. In 1841–42, the master tailor Johann Jakob Senn bought the properties. He pulled down the houses, and built the Hotel Les Trois Rois, whose façade and outline still remain today.

Today

The Hotel Les Trois Rois is now one of the oldest hotels in Europe.

The lodging provided for travellers has always been an important basis for trade, cultural exchange, and the development of society as a whole. The most important hostels were the guesthouses attached to monasteries or convents. Pilgrims and the poor had a right to two to three days of free care and charity. The development of crafts and guilds also meant that a few houses were opened that were the equivalent of hostels. But they were open only to guild members or their guests. From the fourteenth century onwards, there were inns or taverns, with signage outside them as required by the authorities; these were private guesthouses in which locals and strangers could pay for lodgings, food, and drink.

• • •

In 1477, the masters of Basel's guilds issued a list of "Regulations for Innkeepers", as well as laying down rules on hygiene, the minimum price for a meal, the tax due on goods bought, and the safeguarding of morals in inns. The list also included some of the basic rules of gastronomy:
— The innkeepers have the right to store wine in their houses, and to set it before their guests but they may under no circumstances sell wine outside the house.
— The innkeepers should buy fish and meat in the public fish market, and in the slaughterhouse, and it should be fresh, clean, pure, and smell good.
— The innkeepers are not allowed to buy bread from barrows or baskets carried on the back nor are they allowed to accept it for the repayment of debts. They must buy it freshly baked from the shop. If they bake their own bread, they must pay a tax on it.

• • •

Candles and oil lamps were the absolute norm in all first-class hotels through the second half of the nineteenth century. In 1851 a wax candle in the Hotel Drei Könige cost one franc compared to a room price of two francs – quite a steep surcharge given that a candle did not exactly contribute much to the optimal illumination of a room. The first indication that there was electrical light in the hotel is from the year 1898. In 1844, as a result of rebuilding work, Drei Könige had running water on every floor. The water was pumped from the basement up to tanks on the fourth floor, and then distributed via a pipeline. On the floors with guest rooms, the pipeline flowed into a water chamber from where the servants brought guests water to their rooms. Three bathrooms in the basement were available for use by guests, and there were four toilets on each floor. These were arranged around the light and air shafts and emptied into sewers that flowed directly into the Rhine.

• • •

In the nineteenth century a *table d'hôte* of distinction offered:
— First course: Soup, cooked beef, vegetables with lamb, one platter of fried trout, one pastry of chicken with morels, two platters of salad, one platter of Spanish sausages.
— Second course: Three young turkeys, one hare, one leg of mutton, six doves, one platter of cooked trout, two platters chicken fricassee, one platter of artichoke pastry.
— Third course: Fresh fruit, almond tart, one platter with cake or waffles and tobacco rolls, pyramid of sweetmeats, two bowls of preserves, two plates of candies, cheese.

• • •

Basel, with its world-famous art collections, galleries and the Art Basel fair, has always attracted art lovers and artists from all over the world. The following episode is an eloquent illustration of Basel as a city of art: back in the Swinging Sixties, the Kunstmuseum Basel was given the choice of either rustling up 8.4 million francs to buy two famous masterpieces by Pablo Picasso that were on loan to it, or losing them forever. The two pieces were *The Two Brothers* and the *Seated Harlequin*. An extraordinary, popular movement by people of all ages and social backgrounds, supported by the city government, raised the money. Picasso was touched by the enthusiasm shown for his work, and donated four paintings which have enriched the Kunstmuseum ever since. About the hotel, Picasso commented: "I stood on the balcony there a whole night long. The hotel is called the Drei Könige, and is situated on the Rhine. The view is very beautiful. I have never seen such a black river, inky black."

• • •

The experience with the Rolling Stones in the 1980s was special: the porters had never before had to carry so much luggage. It took four of them three hours to bring all the suitcases up to their rooms. The Stones had booked the entire first floor of the hotel for themselves. And then some of them jumped into the Rhine from the ground-floor balcony to cool themselves down. That caused something of a furore.

Whitechapel Bell Foundry
UK

Britain's oldest manufacturing company is responsible for the production of bells including America's Liberty Bell and Big Ben at the Palace of Westminster.

1570

An entry in the Guinness Book of Records lists the Whitechapel Bell Foundry as Britain's oldest manufacturing company, having been established in 1570 and in continuous business since that date.

The Foundry's main business is bellcasting and the manufacture of church bells, their fittings and accessories, although it also makes single bells for tolling, carillon bells, and handbells.

Worldwide export began at an early date. A set of bells was sent to St. Petersburg, Russia in 1747, the first transatlantic delivery was a change ringing peal sent to Christ Church, Philadelphia in 1754, and bells were supplied to St. Michael's Church, Charleston, South Carolina in 1764.

Whitechapel's most famous bells include the original Liberty Bell (1752), the Great Bell of Montreal, and Big Ben at the Palace of Westminster. Cast in 1858, Big Ben is the largest bell ever manufactured at Whitechapel Bell Foundry, weighing thirteen-and-a-half tons.

Today

The present premises on Whitechapel Road and Plumbers Row date from 1670 and formerly housed a coach inn called *The Artichoke*, which closed in 1738.

Despite being such an old, established company, improvements and innovations are always being made by Whitechapel: these include the design and construction of radial frames for change ringing peals, and new technologies in clapper and headstock design, which improve the mechanical properties of church bells. The traditions of craftsmanship and old skills combined with modern technology enable the Whitechapel Bell Foundry in London's East End to produce bells that are still renowned for their quality.

ALAN & KATHRYN HUGHES
Owners and Managing Directors

At a meeting of the Pennsylvania Provincial Assembly in 1751, the Superintendents were instructed to procure a bell of about 2,000 lbs in weight from England. The bell is recorded as having come ashore in good order. A report from 1753 states that after hanging, it became cracked at the first stroke. Good bell metal is extremely brittle: metal up to one inch in thickness can be broken in the palm of the hand by a sharp tap with a two lb hammer. If a bell is struck and not allowed to ring freely, because either the clapper or some part of the frame or fittings are in contact with the bell, then a crack can very easily develop. With the threat of British occupation of Philadelphia in 1777, the Liberty Bell and other bells were hastily removed from the city to prevent their falling into British hands, and being made into cannons. The Liberty Bell was hidden for almost a year, and was returned to Philadelphia in 1778 upon the withdrawal of the British.

• • •

In 1844, Parliament decided that the new buildings for the Houses of Parliament should incorporate a tower and clock. The Astronomer Royal was appointed to draft specifications for the clock. One of his requirements was that "the first stroke of the hour bell should register the time, correct to within one second per day and, furthermore, that it should telegraph its performance twice a day to Greenwich Observatory, where a record would be kept." They turned to the Whitechapel Foundry… The bells of the Great Clock of Westminster rang across London for the first time in 1859, and Parliament had a special sitting to decide on a suitable name for the great hour bell. During the course of the debate, many suggestions were made. Chief Lord of the Woods and Forest, Sir Benjamin Hall, a large and ponderous man known affectionately in the House as *Big Ben*, rose and gave an impressively long speech on the subject. At the end of this oratorical marathon, as Sir Benjamin sank back into his seat, a wag in the chamber shouted out: "Why not call him Big Ben and be done with it?" The House erupted in laughter; Big Ben had been named. This, at least, is the most commonly accepted story…

• • •

To many people around the world, the name Whitechapel evokes not only visions of the bells which the foundry has been producing for many centuries, but also stories about Jack the Ripper and the terrible events of 1888. In the 1880s, Whitechapel was synonymous with crime and poverty; the overcrowded and unsanitary conditions also ensured that disease and infections were endemic. The residents of Whitechapel did whatever was necessary to make ends meet, and many of the women of the area worked as prostitutes in order to pay for a bed for the night rather than, as many people did, live in sewers and fight the rats for whatever sustenance was available. Whitechapel had over 1400 known prostitutes, eighty brothels and countless pubs; little wonder that alcoholism was rampant. Into this wretched stew came Jack the Ripper. He butchered all of his victims at sites no more than ten minutes' walk from the foundry. All of the employees were questioned by the police during their door-to-door enquiries, as were all residents of the area.

• • •

Like most parts of the nation's heavy engineering sector, the Whitechapel Bell Foundry's manufacturing capacity was turned to war-related production in times of conflict. The similarity of bell metal and gunmetal, and the ease with which one can be melted down and turned into the other – which is the reason why an enemy's bells were long considered one of the prizes of war – means that the foundry has been involved in producing cannons at various times. During the Second World War, the foundry was given orders by the British government to produce aluminium castings of submarine parts for the Admiralty. The government not only guaranteed the orders, but it also guaranteed good prices and quick payment, which is something that the Church of England has never managed to do!

• • •

The Whitechapel Bell Foundry designed the Olympic Bell, which was used for the opening ceremony of the 2012 Olympic Games in London. The furnaces at Whitechapel could not provide the twenty-three tons of molten metal required to make the bell, so it was manufactured at a factory in the Netherlands, which normally produces ship propellers.

THE ESSENCE OF THIS BOOK IS DESCRIBED BY THE
FASHION DESIGNER NICOLAS GHESQUIÈRE IN THE
FOLLOWING WORDS: "IT IS VITAL TO SHOWCASE
HERITAGE BRANDS IN TODAY'S CLIMATE."